On the Greens of Massachusetts

THE STORY OF THE
WOMEN'S GOLF ASSOCIATION OF MASSACHUSETTS
1900-2000

Library of Congress Cataloging-in-Publication Data

Women's Golf Association of Massachusetts (WGAM)
On the Greens of Massachusetts
The Story of the Women's Golf Association of Massachusetts
1900 – 2000

1st edition
ISBN 0-9716300-0-3

Author of Part I – The Story, Moira McCarthy
Edited by Dawn Ciardi and Kathleen Ring James
Cover and interior design by Kathleen B. Branigan
Front Cover Photo: Mrs. Raymond July 1904, Copyright – Robert L. Stewart, Frame Central

Printed in the United States of America

DEDICATION

This book is dedicated to the countless volunteers of the
Women's Golf Association of Massachussets.

*"Golf isn't just about hitting balls. There's a lot more to it in
terms of respect for the traditions of the game, and ultimately,
giving something back."*

Edwina Hughes
Executive Committee Member (13 years)

ACKNOWLEDGEMENTS

This book was completed with the help of many people to whom the Women's Golf Association of Massachusetts is deeply grateful. Special recognition is given to the Women's Golf Association of Massachusetts' Centennial Book Committee members who generously contributed of their time and energy for more than two years:

Jan Bath
Carolyn Boday
Elna Carlson
Sally Foehl
Louise Mariani
Suzanne Nelson
Judith Norton
Pippy O'Connor

TABLE OF CONTENTS

Introduction

Jeanne-Marie Boylan
USGA Executive Committee Member

The centenary of the Women's Golf Association of Massachusetts is an appropriate time to reflect on the people and events that literally transformed the game of golf well beyond the geographical boundaries of the Commonwealth of Massachusetts. While it is not possible to chronicle the struggles and accomplishments of all involved in the development of women's golf, this commemorative publication does characterize both the times in which Massachusetts women's golf evolved and the women whose golf skills, tenacity and commitment are admired to this day.

Not surprisingly it all began as many great movements do: a small group of people demonstrating passion for a cause, trying to accomplish the seemingly impossible. While the game of golf is not typically associated with great causes, it is not inappropriate to view it in this context, especially if we are mindful of the societal changes that paralleled the growth of women's golf and in many ways were responsible for it as well as influenced by it. At the turn of the century it took a combination of courage and self-confidence to challenge the male-dominated culture characterized by some very stereotypically male ideas about the appropriate behavior of a "lady". This image of ladies did not include forcefully swinging at a golf ball nor tackling the logistics of solitary travel to New York or Philadelphia for competitions.

It all started when six women gathered for tea one afternoon on Commonwealth Avenue and admittedly, unceremoniously laid the groundwork for what would become the Women's Golf Association of Boston. These founders were determined and brave. Indeed, they persisted and established an organization three years before their male counterparts. These were forward thinking "ladies" who realized they were stepping into a new arena of both camaraderie and competition that would present challenges. Not only did they set a standard for future generations but, equally significant, they provided the inspiration for those who followed. The founders of the WGAB not only cared about their golf games, but also distinguished themselves by their civic contributions. They were always willing to focus the attention of the membership on those in need, through such activities as raising money for the American Red Cross during World War I, contributing to the Unemployment Relief Fund during the depression years and supporting the Allied troops in Europe during World War II.

Our story begins to unfold in Chapter One. As readers, we are invited to enter the parlor of Mrs. Charlotte Gannett Wells in 1900 and overhear conversations that would change the world of golf and status of women for generations to come. We follow these women as they play in the first matches of the newly formed Women's Golf Association of Boston and vicariously witness play on the day of their first championship. We watch as more clubs join the association. Three years later, at another parlor meeting, this time at the home of Mrs. A. B. Cobbs, a total of thirty clubs could be counted as WGAB members. During this period, we are also introduced to the Curtis sisters, Margaret and Harriot, and begin to gain an appreciation of their unparalleled roles — spanning decades — that advanced women's golf as well as women's amateur sports.

In 1920 with the ratification of the Nineteenth Amendment came a fresh wave of consciousness about the expanded role of women in society. The effect upon the WGAB was no less momentous as noted in Chapter Two, when members attempted to balance their desire to play and advance women's golf, fully aware this sport was undeniably a game dominated by men. Yet, while men continued to control access to golf courses, women's golf was beginning to gain recognition. This was due in great measure to the dedication of the Curtis sisters, who won the U.S. Women's Amateur four times between them. After participating in informal international matches since 1905, in 1927 the sisters donated a cup to the United States Golf Association inscribed, "To stimulate friendly rivalry among the women golfers of many lands". It was in no small part due to their persistence that the United States Golf Association officially sanctioned the Curtis Cup Match in 1932. The recognition of the first women's international competition between teams from the United States and Great Britain and Ireland fulfilled the resolve of the sisters to promote international goodwill through friendly competition. The influence of the Curtis sisters was not confined solely to golf with overseas neighbors. Recognizing that youth were the future of the game, Margaret advocated beginning a junior girls' championship in Massachusetts. Her efforts were rewarded and by the end of the decade, WGAB numbers swelled and membership had to be limited only to Massachusetts' golfers. In recognition of this unprecedented growth and statewide membership, the Boston-based organization was renamed the Women's Golf Association of Massachusetts.

We learn more about the civic-minded Curtis sisters and their influence throughout World War II in the third chapter. They led the WGAM in efforts to support troops abroad, organizing donations to purchase a mobile kitchen in Britain and collecting golf balls to send to the troops for recreation. Meanwhile, at home during the war years, many women worked, some for the first time, and increasingly devel-

oped new skills of self-confidence and self-sufficiency. This newfound independence, in turn, led more women to engage in previously male dominated pastimes such as golf.

In Chapter Four, entitled "Mid-Century", the events of the 50th anniversary are described. After 50 years of existence, the WGAM saw a dramatic shift in both recognition and growth. As more women flocked to the fairways, new events were added to the calendar. The efforts to establish junior programs and attract more girls to the game were reaping benefits and at the same time the WGAM Senior Championship was flourishing. Women's golf was receiving increasing national recognition and in Massachusetts the competition was keener than it had ever been before.

The fifth chapter chronicles the 1960s and 1970s, periods that witnessed continued WGAM growth and renewed challenges to provide access to courses for the increasing numbers of women who had taken up the game. The leaders of women's golf in Massachusetts were gaining respect in our country and abroad. Mildred Prunaret followed in the footsteps of the Curtis sisters. Having served as President of the Women's Golf Association of Massachusetts, Mrs. Prunaret went on to assume the Chair of the United States Golf Association's Women's Committee, became Captain of the 1960 United States Curtis Cup Team, was an original organizer of the Women's World Amateur Team Championship and served as Captain of the United States Women's World Amateur Team in 1970. Thus, Massachusetts women played significant roles in the creation of both the Curtis Cup and the Women's World Amateur Team Championship, the only international team events for women

conducted by the United States Golf Association.

Chapter Six recalls what for many of us is modern history. During the 1980s and 1990s the WGAM flourished, providing opportunities for competition and camaraderie. The difficult task of securing golf courses for tournaments, which had been faced by the founders, continued to challenge the new leadership. The composition of the membership was changing as several prominent golfers moved from the amateur ranks to teach or play professionally. Ironically, increasing numbers of women in the workforce created a void of younger women participating in WGAM events. Recognizing that the future of women's golf was in jeopardy, the WGAM renewed its efforts to introduce junior girls to the game of golf. The civic nature of the WGAM membership was once again evident as the Dolly Sullivan Tournament and the WGAM Junior Scholarship Fund were established to support the pursuit of higher education by young women involved in golf. With the support of the WGAM and many others they have been successful in their mission.

The seventh and final chapter, aptly titled "Champions, Legends and Ambassadors", depicts individuals who are well known in WGAM circles and offers a compilation of championship information. The "last word" belongs to Jane Frost who delighted us at the Centennial Evening of Champions with her presentation "What Makes A Champion". In her remarks one can identify the characteristics of the women who are responsible for the creation and preservation of the Women's Golf Association of Massachusetts.

As I conclude this introduction, I must take a moment to reflect on my own association with the WGAM. I was fortunate to be a participant in WGAM events for six years during the 1970s. As a newcomer to competitive golf in 1972, I especially appreciated the superior level of competition and the strong bonds that developed among competitors. WGAM events offered serious competition on challenging golf courses and the summer revolved around "the State". I learned about the legacy we inherited from the founders of the WGAM and developed a deep respect for all those whose passion for the game had created the opportunity for me to play competitive golf. Attending the WGAM 75th Anniversary celebration during the Association Championship at Weston Golf Club provided an opportunity to see and hear from many of the women who were prominent in Massachusetts golf history. It undoubtedly provided inspiration to fulfill my dream that

week and win the Association Championship. Having served on both WGAM and USGA committees, I have been privileged to work with individuals fully committed to promoting the game of golf and providing the framework for competitions that guarantee a level playing field for all. I have been fortunate to be involved in a game that is characterized by self-discipline and integrity and believe that those who experience the game can be beneficiaries of the tremendous lessons golf provides about respect for one another.

The six women who started it all in March 1900 may not have been able to look through the door that they thrust open to see into the 21st century. Indeed, they probably could not fathom that more than five million women would be playing golf in 2000. They may not have foreseen that the progression of women's golf through the twen-

tieth century would be a precursor to the integration of women into today's society. What they did know was that they wanted to play. They knew that the game of golf would create opportunities for their personal growth. Perhaps most importantly, they enjoyed it. Further, they believed that women deserved the same access to this great sport as anyone else. They were remarkable women, pioneers whose commitment to the game of golf outweighed the often-disparaging comments and glances from friends and family. Their courage and conviction can most aptly be captured by quoting Margaret Mead, another woman born ahead of her time and recognized as a champion in her field. "Never doubt that a small group of thoughtful, committed citizens can change the world. Indeed, it is the only thing that ever has."

Jeanne-Marie Boylan
Executive Committee
United States Golf Association

Part One

The Story

The Beginning

"The manner in which they took hold of the matter and organized the association . . . and the way in which it has been conducted, free from debt and without outside assistance which could have been had at any time, speaks volumes for the sportsmanship involved, and affords a fine example for the men of Boston to follow."

The Transcript Newspaper, Oct. 27, 1900

At least on the surface, the scene was likely repeating itself in many of the brickfront homes dotting Boston's Back Bay that turn-of-the-century day. Six women, well dressed in floor-sweeping, waist-pinching dresses, sat in the palatial parlor of Mrs. Charlotte Gannett Wells and exchanged small talk — the children, their husband's latest sporting conquest, the latest efforts at training the household help, what Godey's was saying the next fashion would be. Tea steeped in the kitchen, ready for a soon-needed break. They were society ladies, doing what they were expected to do.

That all changed when Miss Grace Keyes of Concord set both hands on her knees, leaned forward and brought up the subject the women had agreed to meet about. Her words and this meeting would alter their lives forever.

"What we want, what we need," she said, looking each in the eye, "is a way to play and improve at golf. We need more chances to play and compete. We need to meet other women who love golf as well." The other women nodded in solidarity.

At that meeting, a revolution was launched. Not a battle, mind you, just a long march toward what is now the Women's Golf Association of

Massachusetts, one of the most respected and successful golf groups of its kind. Good golf and plenty of it has indeed been the outcome of that society tea, more than Miss Keyes ever dreamed. Back then, she was just hoping for a few organized rounds.

Women's golf was in its infancy on that day — March 5, 1900. While history can trace women golfers back to the year 1567, it is only a mere mention. One of the first well-known women golfers was Mary Queen of Scots, who coined the phrase "caddie" when she used cadets to send messages to the castle while she played golf.

In Scotland by the late 19th century, golf for women was a known element. The fabled St. Andrews founded a women's golf club in 1867, and England followed suit with the Westward Ho! Ladies' Golf Club the next year. The rage swept Europe. In 1893, the first Ladies' Golf Championship was held by the newly formed Ladies' Golf Union in England. Men clearly felt that while it might be amusing to see women hit a few, competition for women on the links seemed far-fetched. Said one British golf official of the upcoming

event, "Tears will bedew, if wigs do not bestrew, the green." The women proved him wrong, turning in respectable (although high by today's standards) scores. Women's golf was here to stay.

Boston, however, was a holdout. Not that women weren't playing golf in the States — they were. *The New York Times* made note of a women's driving contest in 1897. The winner drove 137 yards. That same year, *Ladies Home*

*45 Commonwealth Avenue
Boston, Massachusetts*

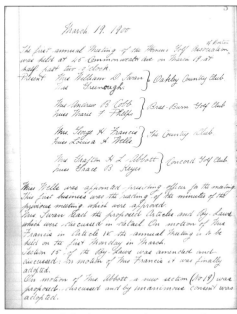

Minutes of the meeting held at 45 Commonwealth Avenue, on March 5, 1900, "for the purpose of forming a Golf Association among women".

Journal suggested that "middle aged women" learn golf as a great form of diversionary exercise. Still, the sport was slow to catch on, with clubs landing for the most part only in the hands of the wives and daughters of post Civil-War-era millionaires.

Miss Florence Boit was one such golfer. When she came to visit her aunt and uncle, the Hunnewells of Wellesley, she brought her clubs with her. Since there were no golf courses in the Boston area in the late 19th century, her uncle set about building three holes for her on his sprawling grounds. Neighbors soon came to watch the spectacle of a woman playing golf. One was Laurence Curtis, who was so taken by the event, he convinced his beloved Country Club in Brookline to give golf a chance. They built their first six holes the following

year. His nieces, Harriot and Margaret Curtis, were soon to make a major impact on the sport as well.

Massachusetts' men, and a smattering of women, took to the game at The Country Club as well as at Essex, Brae Burn, Oakley and Concord. By the turn of the century, more than a select few women were playing golf in the state, yet they were still an anomaly. The six women who met together wanted to be part of a larger golf scene.

They all agreed: For women to improve as golfers, they would need friendly competition and camaraderie. Finding that would require organization, cooperation and a little bit of a push. They agreed to go back to the ladies who frequented their clubs and look for joiners. With no set name nor any real idea of what might develop, they planned to meet again on March 19 to see if they had any support. Tea was poured and like the good Back Bay women they were, the ladies sat straight in their chairs and sipped slowly. But the small talk had changed. Golf had just become their life.

❧

Their friends did follow. Two weeks later on March 19 of that same year in that same parlor, eight women met and promptly at half past the hour of two o'clock voted to form the Women's Golf Association of Boston (WGAB). With Wells presiding as interim president, they voted in officers: Mrs. Franz Zerrahn of The Country Club as President, Mrs. William Swan of Oakley as Vice

President, Louisa Wells of The Country Club as Secretary and Miss Grace Keyes of Concord Golf Club as Treasurer. They then voted to hold an annual meeting each March, an Association Championship in the autumn and to arrange Team Matches to give the women a chance to play regularly. With the four member clubs, they set up a grid of Team Matches and agreed to meet on the links May 2, 1900 to tee off as an Association for the first time. With no men's association in Massachusetts, the women would find they would not be an anomaly for long; they would be leaders.

Some curious spectators took in the scene at The Country Club the morning of May 2, 1900. Sixteen women were set to tee off as the four teams of the WGAB played their first Team Matches. Each team would play six matches that year, three on their home course and three away and the winner would hold

Minutes of the first annual meeting of the Women's Golf Association of Boston, March 19, 1900.

the Team Championship Cup. Any team to win three years in a row would keep the Cup for good.

The women, in their long, binding dresses, felt the heat of that sunny spring day almost immediately. Swinging wasn't easy in those flowing skirts, but they took to it like champs. It was clear from the outset of this debut season that one team would dominate. Of the four member clubs: Oakley, Brae Burn, Concord and The Country Club, it was clear Oakley would rule, Concord challenge them, The Country Club hold their own and Brae Burn struggle. In fact, that first match between The Country Club and Brae Burn ended in a shutout, with The Country Club taking all 32 points and Miss Louisa Wells winning 11 of those single-handedly. That same day at Watertown, Oakley beat Concord 19-2. But one week later, The Country Club was to learn the true meaning of home club advantage when Concord whipped them 24 to 5 on the Concord course.

Win or lose, closely contested or edged out, one thing was certain: these women were immediately hooked on competitive golf. They could not get enough, which in the early 20th century male dominated world wasn't easy. For the most part, these women fell into two categories: wives of successful millionaires or wealthy single women. The reason was obvious: for a woman to be a golfer, she either had full-time in-home help or she didn't have children. And so the roots of women's golf are embedded in wealth. That's not to say these

women were indulgent. They ran the WGAB well, taking in only the minimal amount of money they needed and making every penny stretch as far as it could. By the time the Association Championship rolled around in late October, word was out via the press and the club gentlemen: the WGAB was a success in every way possible.

"The frequent visiting of other links than their own, the meeting of other golfers and the stimulus of match play has had a most beneficial effect upon women's golf," one newspaper columnist wrote at the start of the

MISS GRACE B. KEYES, WINNER OF THE CHAMPIONSHIP OF THE WOMEN'S GOLF ASSOCIATION.

Association Championship. "They have increased in proficiency in a far greater proportion than have the men of the Boston district." To those six founding women, it was music to their ears. To the 40 participants in that first Association Championship at Oakley Country Club Oct. 22-25, it was a call to action.

☙❧

Mother Nature has a way of saying thank you in New England. She chooses one October day, and it's usually just one, and paints it perfect. Blue skies dotted by white, puffy clouds offset the brilliant oranges and yellows of the tall trees. There's a breeze, but only enough to make you comfortable in your autumn wear. The sun beats warm on your face, but you still need a sweater. Such was the weather delivered to the WGAB on Oct. 22, 1900, the first day of their first Championship. Only one woman defaulted that glorious autumn day, and that default was because of illness. The remaining 39 women arrived at Oakley early and eager for the first ever championship. Readied by a Team Match series that ended, as expected, with Oakley winning the cup, the women were eager to show how much their games had improved. The women of Brae Burn, who suffered huge defeats in the most sportsmanlike of ways all season, were particularly keyed up.

The first pair teed off promptly at 9:45 a.m., with the last going off, as planned, exactly at noon. With no wind, a warm "Indian Summer" sun and a course in perfect condition, the women played at their best. It was clear by the buzz at lunchtime, the exhilaration of competition had lifted them all.

Their faces flushed with the high of great sports, the women held a "competition within a competition" in the form of a putting and approaching contest. A simple statewide championship, it seemed, was not enough to whet their appetite for competitive golf.

The putting and approaching contest was held on the 13th hole, known then as "The Elbow." The 16 contestants were allowed three balls to approach and putt out at distances of 25, 35 and 50 yards. As a crowd cheered them on, the contest ended with Marie Phelps of Brae Burn and Mrs. N.C. Sargent of The Country Club in a tiebreaker. Sargent went first, tucking the balls in tight to the pin. Phelps grabbed her chipper and breathed deeply, feeling the long season of Brae Burn losses on her shoulders. Grimacing, she focused on the hole and chipped in to win. It was a minor aside to some, but a huge win for the good sports of Brae Burn.

Still wanting more, the women held a driving contest. They moved onto the 12th hole, known as "The Marble,"

Louisa Wells

where 12 contestants were given three drives each into fairways 45 feet wide. Any drive less than 100 yards would automatically disqualify the player. The total of those three drives would be the final score. Louisa Wells won the event with three drives of 148 1/4, 137 and 114 for a total of 399 1/4. While Pauline Mackay hit the longest single drive of the day — a whalloping 150 1/4 yards — her total only brought her to second place.

Two contest winners were in place and the qualifiers were ready to play on in the tournament, and it was only the end of Monday. The women went home exhilarated, having formed a bond based equally on fun and competition. The only thing they loved more than having fun together was beating one another on the links. There wasn't a doubter in the house or the state: women's golf was here to stay.

The good weather and good luck continued through the week with the first Association Championship going to Grace Keyes of Concord Golf Club, who defeated Harriot Curtis of Oakley Country Club on the 15th, five up with three to play. Keyes held the silver cup high above her head as her fellow women golfers, as well as male spectators, cheered. She was a winner, she knew, but so was her sport. Everyone shared in the victory.

✦-✦

By February of 1901, three more clubs, Vesper in Lowell, Wollaston Golf Club and Lexington Golf Club had joined the

Association. With a membership nearing 100, the group's impact on the area became tangible. The first clear sign of their clout may have been a May, 1901 newspaper advertisement offering a 10 percent discount on clubs and 20 percent off a dozen balls at the Connell and Campbell Company in Boston to any WGAB member.

Another sign of their success was the spring Team Match on May 31, 1901, when Brae Burn, for the first time, actually won a match. They beat Vesper

10-5 and, with the same good sportsmanship they displayed through a losing season, gave warm encouragement to the Vesper women. After all, one might note, the Brae Burn women certainly felt their pain.

The women also decided that while Mother Nature had looked well upon them at their first Association Championship, holding the tournament in late fall in New England might be risky. So the second championship was set for June, this time at The Country Club. The weather was indeed delightful, and so was the drama of the event,

"Still, there is sport to be had when one does not aspire to become even a 'local champion' and with the idea of promoting the game, giving an opportunity for team matches and bringing about rivalry in the sport."

—-*Grace Keyes, 1907*

BOSTON WOMEN TAKE EVERY GOLF HONOR

Misses Osgood, Adams and Mackay and Mrs. Batchelder Win at Nassau.

[Special Dispatch to the Boston Herald.]

NEW YORK, June 8, 1906. Miss Fanny Osgood, twice champion of the Women's Boston Golf Association, won the first woman's eastern championship at the Nassau County Club today. The conditions called for two rounds at medal play, a match on succeeding days. At the first attempt Miss Osgood completed the 6000-yard round in 88, two strokes behind Miss Louise Vanderhoef, and a stroke better than Miss Harriot Curtis and Mrs. Caleb Fox, who tied for third place. Continuing today, Miss Vanderhoef, after sailing along merrily for seven holes, was put completely off her game. As a result, she finished in 97, or 183 for the two rounds.

Miss Osgood, on the other hand, very wisely took no chances, and, playing with great "economical" judgment, she was content to go out in 45 and home in similar figures. Second to her was Mrs. Ronald H. Barlow, the Philadelphia champion, who, with a round of 85, finished in 180, or two strokes behind the winner.

Miss Harriott Curtis finished third, a stroke behind Mrs. Barlow and just one ahead of her sister, Margaret Curtis. The last named was fourth and Miss Louise Vanderhoef tied for fifth place with Mrs. Caleb Fox.

Miss Fanny Osgood, Brookline—
Out..... 4 7 4 5 6 5 4 5 5—45
In....... 5 3 5 5 6 7 5 5 4—45—90
First day's total, 88—178.

The other scores:
Mrs. R. H. Barlow, Merion, 91, 89, 180; Miss H. Curtis, Essex, 89, 92, 181; Miss M. Curtis, Essex, 92, 90, 182; Miss L. Vanderhoef, Ardsley, 86, 97, 183; Mrs. C. F. Fox, Huntingdon Valley, 89, 94, 183; Mrs. C. T. Stout, Richmond County, 95, 91, 186; Miss G. Bishop, Brooklawn, 94, 92, 186; Miss P. Mackay, Oakley, 94, 93, 187; Miss M. S. Adams, Wollaston, 91, 97, 188; Miss L. A. Wells, Brookline, 95, 95, 190; Miss Julia Mix, Englewood, 95, 99, 194; Miss E. Lockwood, Lexington, 96, 102, 198.

The 26 who failed on the first day to finish within 10 strokes of the leaders continued for a cup under handicap. Mrs. Batchelder of the Weston and Oakley clubs won the net prize with 90. She also tied with Miss Frances Griscom for the gross prize with a card of 95, but waived all claim to the latter. By Mrs. Batchelder's victory Boston won every competition of the two days' meeting, and Miss "Mollie" Adams led in the driving contest, and Miss Pauline Mackay, after a tie with the former, the approaching and putting contest.

---

with Margaret Curtis showing everyone why her name was becoming synonymous with national golf.

In only the second round of play, Curtis treated onlookers to a real nail-biter, taking a win from M.B. Adams of Wollaston on the 21st hole. In the semi-finals, Curtis defeated Mackay, this time on the 19th. She trounced defending champ Keyes in the final. However, with those early sudden death matches, the tradition of tense championship moments began.

As for the approach and putting contests, the women showed their grit

Miss Fannie Osgood Association Champion in 1903, 1904, 1910, 1911 and 1913.

> Massachusetts women dominated the finals of the U.S. Women's Amateur Championship for three consecutive years. Pauline Mackay defeated Margaret Curtis in 1905, Harriot Curtis defeated Mary B. Adams in 1906, and Margaret Curtis defeated Harriot Curtis in 1907.

again, saying they didn't want it to be too easy. They chose the second hole, an approach that obliged them to hit up and over a bunker. Challenge was the name of the game in every way possible for these women.

Also in 1901, the WGAB decided to look beyond their borders for even more camaraderie and competition. They wrote to the Women's Metropolitan Golf Association of New York and New Jersey and challenged them to a match some time in the upcoming year. In return, they were invited to join the Inter-City competition, which had begun in 1898 between the Women's Metropolitan Association and the Women's Golf Association of Philadelphia. Their first go at that would come in 1902. But first, in the summer of 1901, the Women's Championship of the United States Golf Association (USGA) was held at The Country Club. With 92 entrants and 32 qualifiers, the event attracted huge crowds. But locals could have seen about the same play on any Spring Match day since 12 of the 32 qualifiers were from the Boston area. And 10 of those were WGAB members, an impressive number when you realize there were still only seven member clubs. Indeed, the *Herald* noted that being a champ in Boston was more than a regional honor, saying, "A player who wins the Boston championship is regarded as nearly as important a personage as the national titleholder." The *Transcript* echoed that, saying of the Association Championship, "The strongest field yet mustered in a purely state event, and fully as good, if not better, than could be assembled in any other part of the country." The WGAB was making its mark nationally, never mind locally.

In the fall of 1902 came the biggest competition; the match the women of the WGAB eagerly anticipated— the Clement Acton Griscom Inter-City Cup, played that year at The Baltusrol Golf Club in Short Hills, New Jersey. The Massachusetts women trained hard and hand picked a team they felt would represent not only the best in Boston, but the best anywhere. Word had gotten out that the cream of the golf crop was in Boston. Now the women would have a chance to prove it. They did so on October 29, trouncing Philadelphia 44 to 11 to earn the right to challenge the Metropolitan Association, who had won the Cup the year before. The next day, the WGAB team beat New York 32 to 18 and took the Griscom Cup for the first time. The cream had risen to the top.

On January 21, 1903 the WGAB held an informational meeting for women and clubs interested in joining. Held at the home of Mrs. A.B. Cobbs at the Westgate in Boston, 27 clubs were represented. By the March 3 annual meeting, 30 clubs were signed on as members and those six women who met at the Back Bay home knew for sure they were getting what they wished for: competitive golf and camaraderie.

❖❖

More and more women were joining the golf force and those who were already in it became more committed to the sport they loved. It wasn't easy to

---

HOLIDAY SHOPPING MADE EASY

While the equipment of the early 1900's was primitive at best compared to the graphite magic wands of today, there were gizmos aplenty, making holiday shopping for the lady golfer in your life a breeze. Some items in existence in the early 1900's include:

❖ The Pick-up: An early version of the shag bag used to scoop up practice balls.

❖ Tethered practice balls: A golf ball tied to an elasticized rope just in case you don't want to bother with the Pick-up bag.

❖ Hand held ball cleaner: To keep your balls shiny no matter where you are on the course.

❖ Practice putting mat: Patented at the turn of the century, still a holiday gift staple.

❖ True White Balls: Introduced by Spalding in 1905, they were all the rage.

---

commit, (consider just the logistics of getting back and forth from the golf course with no automobiles), but the women found that golf and competition indeed bettered their lives and was worth the effort. Said Grace Keyes in 1907, the combination of women and golf could only make the world a better place. "There are few games better adapted to teaching women what it is to

> **"The Championship had a fatal effect last year for the champion was married! Beware!"**
>
> *Mrs. Wheeler on M. L. Adams Championship*
> *win and soon-to-follow marriage in 1909.*

become a 'good sport' than golf. A great many people differ in the opinion as to whether women should have muscle, but in these days when they enter so

many of the occupations of men, is it not well to see what they may also do to keep their physical condition up to something better than the hysteria point?"

Her words were well heeded among the women at the 1907 annual meeting. The turn of the century had brought more women into extended education, some even into career paths. The golf course was just one of the many places considered taboo for ladies by conservatives of both sexes. And far from "becoming hysterical" in moments of crisis, women were showing, on the course, just how levelheaded and flexible they could be. Take this as a case in point: For the 1906 Griscom Cup, Boston sent a team by train to Nassau Country Club, no small feat in those days. The night before the big match against Philadelphia they realized that they were one player short due to illness. Rather than hand the cup over to Philadelphia, the Boston Team wired Miss Alice Underwood of Oakley, who hopped a train at the last minute and found her way southwest to the club, arriving just at the moment she should tee off. It was then she realized that, in her hasty rescue mission, she'd left her clubs in Boston. Undeterred, she borrowed clubs and set out to play a course she'd never laid eyes on with clubs she'd never touched before. She played valiantly, but lost on the 19th hole, giving her opponent a good run for her money.

They didn't back down to weather either. For the 1907 championship, held May 21-25 at Woodland Golf Club in Auburndale, nature whipped up a frenzy of rain, sleet, and cold. The women

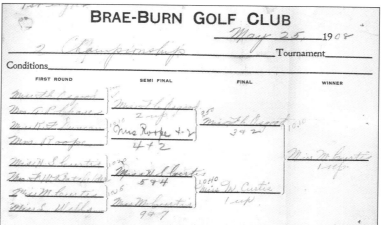

Match Play Draw — Brae-Burn Golf Club, May 25, 1908

played through it all, prompting one reporter to write, "The bedraggled appearance of the skirts after 18 holes of play indicated that the conditions if anything were worse underfoot than overhead." There was no question; golf and women were meshing well. The annual report of 1905 perhaps said it best. "By these tournaments, many new players were brought face to face with themselves and found themselves real golfers."

✦✦

By the middle of the decade, the WGAB had shown steady growth and even had the need to divide golfers into classes A, B and C. The Curtis sisters were the golf sensations of the nation, but still fully active in the WGAB. It was at an Executive Committee meeting on April 28, 1917

that the Curtis sisters, stunned and saddened by the start of World War I, convinced the Association to double the championship entrance fee to $2 and give half to the Metropolitan Boston Chapter of the American Red Cross. The group also voted to not play in the Inter-City Griscom Cup and to hold no Eastern Championships, all because of the brewing war. That year's Championship Tournament was held on June 4-7 and, when the champions too donated their prizes to the pot for the Red Cross, a total of $173.50 was raised for the cause.

One year later, the WGAB experienced their own war-related tragedy. Miss Dorothy Crosby, an active WGAB member and excellent golfer, enlisted as a nurse to care for soldiers. She was in training at a hospital in Ayer taking care of influenza patients in September of 1918 when she contracted the disease and died "giving her life to her country." Crosby was deeply mourned by the entire Association. Said Fanny Osgood, she was "a great sportsman and one of our best players." The women doubled their efforts to help the war end, donating all their prize money to the cause. There were no other WGAB casualties noted and with the war's end, competition resumed. Through the hardships they discovered the restorative potential of pleasures like golf.

ONE HOT TEE

Perhaps the most important invention in golf — the wooden golf tee — actually came into existence in Boston. In the beginning, golfers had to use water and sand to form a small mound to set their ball on for tee-off. (In fact, a "good" caddie was one who was expert at making just the right mound). Then Boston dentist George F. Grant, one of the first African Americans ever to play golf and the son of freed slaves, formulated the golf tee as a way to keep his hands clean while playing. His friends loved them, and he made plenty, giving them away by the score. He never patented the item, and someone else came along and mass marketed them. The first big purchase of golf tees went to Woolworths in Boston, where surely many Bay State ladies scooped them up by the dozens.

The Curtis Sisters

Never did a golf club find a more comfortable home, one might say, than in the grip of one of the Curtis sisters. Quiet "Miss Harriot" and her outgoing sister Margaret were talented, eccentric, and dedicated. They were much of the reason why women's golf flourished through the past century.

Born two of ten well-known Curtis children, who wintered on Beacon Hill and summered at "Sharksmouth," their summer home near Essex County Club, Harriot and Margaret took to golf as youngsters. When twelve-year-old Margaret reached the finals of the club championship, someone asked her opponent, "How could you let that child beat you?" The defeated adult shot back, "That's not a child, she's a baby grand." This wasn't the only incidence of resentment of Margaret's prowess and enthusiasm. Once when Margaret made a hole-in-one on a 210-yard hole, she jumped up and down, and screamed, "It's in the hole! It's in the hole!" To which a man watching replied frostily, "After all, that was your objective, wasn't it?"

Margaret qualified for the Women's National Championship at Essex in 1897, but did not win. Harriot became the national champion in 1906, but lost in 1907 when Margaret beat her in the finals. Not a one-sport athlete, Margaret subsequently won the National Women's Doubles Tennis Championships with Elenora Sears in 1908. But it was in golf where Margaret truly excelled; she played in the USGA Women's Amateur Championship 23 times between 1897 and 1947. She won three times – in 1907, 1911, and 1912, was runner-up in 1900 and 1905 and she was the medalist six times.

The sisters lobbied for over two decades before winning their proudest victory: creating the Curtis Cup international golf competition between England and the United States. After years of campaigning, the two women purchased and donated the Cup in 1927. The USGA finally sanctioned the matches in 1932, ten years after inaugurating the men's comparable Walker Cup competition.

The Curtis sisters were focused on more than the thrill of victory. From the beginning, they knew that to grow significantly, the game of golf would have to make its own contributions to the world.

It was "Miss Harriot" who first suggested the WGAB raise funds for the Red Cross and war efforts during the First World War. Margaret worked with refugees in Paris in 1917, and then stayed abroad to assist in establishing health clinics to feed undernourished children in Vienna, Prague and Krakow.

Well before the United States entered World War II, the Curtis sisters convinced the WGAM to raise funds to build a portable soup kitchen to send to England, where their good friends, the Ladies' Golf Union, had been activated to feed British troops.

After the end of World War II, Margaret worked to provide golf therapy for recovering veterans, first putting a program into place at the

Harriot Curtis

Veterans' Hospital in Bedford. The successful idea spread to many hospitals across the nation.

When they weren't active in world affairs, they were working to improve golf, albeit in their own quirky way. Margaret started the junior girls' golf program in Massachusetts, and mothered it like a beloved child until the day she died.

"Miss Harriot" was more subdued but Margaret loved to tell her "Sillybillies," as she called her stories, at annual WGAM events. She was a commanding and endearing "character."

Margaret died on Christmas Day 1965, Harriot two years later. Never have two sisters, and perhaps any women, left more of a mark on women's amateur sports.

Margaret Curtis

<u>More Curtis curiosities:</u>

• Margaret had a mini horse's head mounted on top of her car so she'd be able to pick it out in parking lots.

• Margaret once held 25 local firefighters at bay during a brush fire on her family grounds at Sharksmouth. It seems the firefighters were trained to use the water in their truck and Margaret wanted only the family's private water supply used. She held them back and put the fire out on her own.

• Margaret was known for bringing gift balls, occasionally autographed by her, to WGAM meetings and tournaments. She had a unique way of collecting these balls, rolling along in the high rough at Essex, feeling for balls as she rolled. Some days she found as many as 80 balls in the wee hours before the meetings.

• Traveling in post-war Europe in the autumn of 1946, Margaret faced a novel challenge. Stopped at customs for a suspicious looking bag, she was taken into an office and questioned for hours until they finally believed her claim: that anyone who plays golf as much as she does needs that many pairs of golf cleats. She was let go with her six pairs of shoes intact.

• This is not to imply that fashion was the sisters' forte. Said the Beverly Times in Margaret's obituary after she died on Christmas Day 1965, "Her beat up shoes and sagging socks drew incredulous glances from people who could hardly believe such a great golfer could wear such footgear."

Membership 1900 – 4 Clubs, 30 Members

| 0 | 500 | 1000 | 1500 | 2000 | 2500 |

The Early Years

"It would seem then that what this Association wants above all things is golf and lots of it,"

Mrs. F.A. Stanwood, WGAB Secretary, 1934

The 20's roared for golf as much as they did for anything else in America. The ladies of the WGAB, now firmly entrenched in the sport, found their ranks growing at a rate beyond their wildest dreams. "We have some new and very promising players coming up," Fanny Osgood noted at a meeting in January 1920. The ranks of women golfers were growing in numbers and ability across the nation. If the Boston ladies were to keep their reputation of being the best, they could not afford to become complacent. Thus, the 1920's were launched with a battle plan. Called "The Play Plan," the new program was begun with three goals: to vastly improve play for women on all levels, to raise the level of competition in WGAB events and to win back the Griscom Cup, which had been away from Boston for eight years. "We can this June win back the Inter-City Cup, which has gone on a temporary journey to New York and Philadelphia," Osgood proclaimed at that same meeting.

The plan also called for more matches between teams and a captains' program that kept captains in closer touch with teammates as well as with the WGAB Executive Committee and officers. This would allow the WGAB to see where improvement was needed and which players were dominating.

May 1921 came and the women were ready to roll out the plan full force. New England weather wasn't on their side this time, however.

It rained. And rained. And rained. And while the determined women played through the rain, not canceling a single match, the golf was difficult and not conducive to major improvement. Understanding that such was the life of the New England golfer, the women played on, working to improve their games despite the dismal gray skies every day. They persevered, reminding themselves that at least they were playing the game they loved. "Rain on the Eastern Championships or the Griscom Cup will have no terror for the Boston team," member Elizabeth

The Griscom Cup

Fashion of the day —
Scituate Country Club, 1920

Baldwin noted cheerfully. "This year we have learned all about equipping ourselves both mentally and physically for wet weather."

On June 8-10, 1921 at The Country Club, the chance came to see if their plan was working. The Inter-City Griscom Cup, held at the time by New York, was at stake. With a huge crowd watching and the *Boston Globe* snapping pictures, the ladies, led by the great hope Elizabeth Gordon of Rhode Island

Country Club, took to their home links intent on winning the Cup.

Philadelphia was determined too, winning the first seven of the fifteen matches, where the Boston ladies had expected to get a good lead. The next seven positions played well for Boston and won their matches, leaving the entire weight of the contest on the players in the 15th position. It all rested on the match between Mrs. G.W. Roope of Boston and Mrs. Walter Page of Quaker City. Their match was all even after 18 holes, despite Roope's amazing streak of 13 one-putts in a row. Roope, a good head taller than every other woman out on the course that day, was dressed in a simple white skirt and gray jacket with black piping. The collar of her shirt remained opened while she played, and her gray hat sat still on her head. She fought hard, holding even until the 22nd hole where Page's long putt came close and she then tapped it in for a par. Roope, undeterred by the huge gallery, stepped up to her 22-foot birdie putt and breathed deeply. She read the break, paused over her ball and then stroked it. The ball moved at what seemed the slowest speed ever, rolled directly to the hole and then, the gallery silent, plinked ever so daintily into the cup.

Roope cheered out loud, jumping up and down in a display rare for a woman of that day. As she entered the spacious clubhouse of The Country Club, a hundred-plus other women did the same, screaming out a "standing O" for the lady who had brought the Cup home.

The Play Plan had worked. They were once again on top. And it was a Brae Burn lady, by the way, who put them there.

⋙⋘

Victories seemed to pile high those heady days, and by the end of 1922, the WGAB boasted 40 member clubs and 250 active women golfers. While some of those women had balked at the idea of the tougher spring schedule, they didn't back down from the challenge. A total of 117 women played regularly on the spring teams that year.

In 1922, Boston lost the Griscom Cup again. But they had a bigger national victory when one of their own, Glenna Collett, won the USGA National Championship. She prevailed over 172 national entries with her amazing game, shaped and perfected as a member of the Rhode Island spring team of the WGAB. Collett was able to play in the WGAB by a vote that allowed membership to Rhode Island early on. In late 1922, the WGAB also voted to allow member clubs from Vermont, New Hampshire and Maine as well.

With the swelling of membership and the eyes of the golf world upon them, thanks to the success of "The Play Plan," the women knew that now, more than ever, they needed to set an example to help golf grow as a sport. With that in mind, the WGAB set out to improve members' understanding of the rules, to increase practice among members, and to institute, once and for all, a handicapping system that would make competition in the sport fair and fun.

"A uniform system of handicapping is vital to the best interests of the game of golf," the WGAB wrote in a 1923 resolution declaring that handicapping requirements would be stringent and closely watched. The associations in

New York and Philadelphia followed their lead and did the same.

One month later, a memo was distributed to all WGAB members stressing the importance of rules and etiquette. "The Boston Association should set a high standard in its knowledge of the rules and in its strict observance of these rules," the memo read. "There is no excuse for a breach of any of the rules which come under the Etiquette of Golf. "

The women were convinced that strict observance of rules would be a means to justify their desired end. Rules followed properly lead to less controversy (after all, they thought, how can there be any personal disagreements when rules are there in black and white), and to better play (because, they felt, the rules are there to help you play your best game). The proof of that came on May 23, 1923 at the last event of the spring match season, when 14 players broke 100 on the same day at Belmont Spring Country Club. In that era, this was a major event. Knowledge of the rules, it seemed, brought out the best in the WGAB.

Another accomplishment of national acclaim came two weeks later when Glenna Collett, at the Association Championship, showed the world how drama can play out on a golf course. At The Country Club, her start was dismal. Under blue skies and perfect playing conditions, the national champion hit her second shot on the first hole over the green and into a bunker. On the second hole her long drive went well into the rough. Were that not bad enough, her drive on the third hole sliced into the woods, adding two costly shots.

The crowd was sure the champion was going down, particularly since her opponent that day was another champion, Margaret Curtis. Collett, dressed in a plaid vest and crisp white shirt, touched her brow at her short-cropped hair and vowed to start fresh on the fifth hole. She summoned up all the power she had and shot an amazing round — on in two on the 5th, 9th, 13th, 14th, 15th and 17th — holes men had a difficult time reaching in two in those days. She parred four holes, birdied two, and came in with a 77, a new course record at that time, male or female. "She is every bit the champion," the *Boston Globe* headlines trumpeted. In her photo in the newspaper the next day, she didn't even look winded, but the paper must have felt the need to think a woman would be exhausted after such a feat. The caption below the photo read "The National, Eastern, and North and South title holder sought a soft spot on the club lawn for a mite of a breathing spell." That didn't faze Collett, though, who after winning the Eastern Championship by 11 strokes was treated to this comment by a male columnist: "Her play was quite above being sneezed at." You don't say.

❖

At the same time the handicapping system was luring more women into the game. With 34 as the highest allowed (but marked on cards as 24+), 37 women were enrolled as A players, 48 as

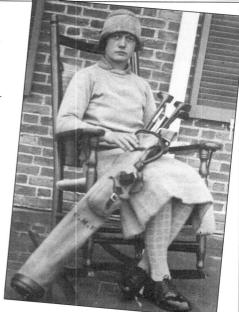
Cris Eaton

RIGHT TRACK, WRONG STATION

Misplacing a club is one thing, misplacing a player is quite another. That's just what happened at the Inter-City Griscom Cup in 1929, played at Aronimink Golf Club in Newtown Square, Pennsylvania. Cris Eaton left instructions to be met at Wayne Junction train station, about 20 miles away from the club. But for some reason, she came through to the Wayside Station, just one mile from the club. When she stepped off the train, no teammate was there to greet her, as was the tradition of the team. Miffed, she found her way to the club, not knowing the entire team was frantically searching for her at Wayne Junction. They finally got together in time for the welcome dinner dance where, notes read, "partners were imported, men of various ages curious to see what the golfing world could produce in the way of dancers." Just don't ask for directions.

B players and 115 as C. With all those players out there, the WGAB had to do something they'd never had to before: limit enrollment in a tournament. The Association Championship that year would be cut off at 18 handicap and lower. Everyone, however, would be invited to compete in the popular side events. The players understood, and played where they could and as often as they could. That was becoming more and more often.

By Christmas of 1924, nearly a quarter century after those six women had

Edith N. Baker - Association Champion 1925, '27, '28, '29, '32

met in Boston, the Association's handicapped players numbered well over 200, and their handicaps were steadily dropping. Osgood, reflecting on the quarter century, said all had gone amazingly well. "There is no doubt that an increasing number of women are playing golf and the standard is rapidly improving."

The fall of 1925 brought in a new tradition for the WGAB, one that lasts to this day. The Connecticut Women's Golf Association challenged Massachusetts to a match. When Massachusetts romped over them 7-2 on October 27, the Connecticut women responded by awarding Massachusetts a beautiful pewter bowl. The WGAB voted to call the bowl the State Team Cup and invited Rhode Island to join the competition. From then on, tri-state matches between Connecticut, Massachusetts and Rhode Island were held. While they put the Cup out in the name of friendship and competition, the Massachusetts women had a feeling they'd be seeing their pewter bowl often. They were right. Over the years, Massachusetts has won a full two-thirds of the time.

By late 1925, the USGA was estimating the population of women golfers in the United States at about 3,000. Close to 500 of them, or nearly 20 percent, were members of the WGAB, residing in and around the Greater Boston area. The USGA looked at the Boston program and agreed the same needed to be done nationally. They set a goal of standardizing handicaps and establishing correct women's par on courses, and encouraging young players to become involved. When a woman golfer suggested starting a USWGA, the USGA agreed to ponder that thought. The USGA then sent a letter to Glenna Collett suggesting women help them in promoting the game. "With careful supervision," the letter read, "it would be possible to show every section of the USA good women's golf at one time or another." Glenna Collett couldn't have agreed more.

✦✦

It was bound to happen sometime, and in the spring of 1926, it did. With

more and more women taking up golf, more and more course time was being devoted to women. That, put simply, bothered the men. "Women golfers and tournaments for women are not altogether regarded with favor by the men, who after all built the courses and pay for them," wrote Eleanor Allen in a memo to the USGA that spring. It wasn't a time when women would even consider they had as much a right as the men to be on the course — women had been voting in America only since 1920. Still, the WGAB knew they wanted to continue to play and grow. They wrote the USGA, asked their advice and suggested a larger, more defined women's USGA committee. The USGA agreed to think it over.

In the meantime, the ladies found themselves, for the first time, at odds with the men of the USGA. It started at the end of 1926 when H. H. Ramsay of the USGA read in a New York newspaper of the Women's Metropolitan Golf Association paying traveling expenses for their Inter-City Griscom Cup team. Boston was doing the same, and Ramsay fired out a note saying the USGA forbade that.

"It is unwise to open the door to the payment of expenses, believing this step would eventually be of serious damage to the associations' well-known regulations and attitude on the subject of amateur status," Ramsay wrote, requesting the associations immediately rescind any travel expense payments they had planned. The Boston women strongly disagreed, and turned to the Massachusetts Golf Association (MGA), the men's group formed in 1903, for guidance. The MGA sided with the USGA, and despite an almost unanimous feeling that paying for the Griscom Cup team travel expenses was the right thing to do for women's amateur golf, the ladies voted to rescind all payments. It was a disappointing loss, but in the 1920's, the women really had no choice. They did, however, make their point, voting at each annual meeting for the remainder of the 1920's a statement saying, "We stand by our former opinion on the subject of paying the expenses of organized teams backed by our association." That declaration was sent to the USGA annually. It would be seven decades before the USGA would reconsider and amend the Rules of Amateur Status to allow players to receive reasonable expenses to represent a golf club or association in a team competition.

At the same time, under the guidance of Margaret Curtis, the WGAB persisted in its efforts to convince the USGA to field an international women's golf competition. Pointing out that men had the Walker Cup, the WGAB urged the USGA to do the same for them. But the USGA, citing financial constraints, refused.

That's not to say the men and women of golf didn't get along. In late 1927, the MGA and WGAB rented their first office space together at 60 State Street, Boston. The shared space allowed both groups to afford a nice setting and to bounce ideas and needs off one another. It was a successful setup and in 2000 the two groups still share office space.

Relationships based on mutual golfing respect were building, too, from male and female participation in the Handicapped Mixed Foursomes Tournament started at Woodland Golf Club in 1924. The tournament, now known as the Stone Cup, quickly became and still remains the quickest field to fill. By 1928, every lady was hoping to play in the popular co-ed event. For those who may have been left out in past years, Fanny Osgood offered advice. "With many saying 'why didn't you play?' and the answer often being 'nobody asked,' our advice is this: to the shy females, since we are in no position to advise the males, ask some hesitating duffer and give him a treat." Many a great golfing duo was formed from that progressive advice.

❦

As the 1920's came near an end and the enrollment forms for membership poured in, the WGAB was faced with a serious decision: should they limit their membership to women playing at clubs in Massachusetts? At an end of the year meeting in 1927, the women sadly voted to do just that, saying the growing numbers left them no choice. They did so, however, with great thanks to the out-of-state teams who had offered them such great support and competition over the years.

"The Providence players have been extremely good sports to come so far so regularly, especially when they have, for

Glenna Collett

the most part, been a losing team," said Margaret Curtis at that meeting.

The decision to allow only Massachusetts members did not ebb the tide of new golfers joining the ranks. By mid 1928, membership stood at 65 clubs and 600 members. This demanded more management than just a volunteer committee. The WGAB voted to staff their new Boston office with their first paid employee — an executive secretary. Mrs. Warren P. Hosmer of Woodland Golf Club was the first, and for a salary of $300 a year, she oversaw the workings of the Association. She was joined shortly after by the second paid employee, a public relations expert at the rate of $100 per year. A finance committee was formed as well, and as the decade closed, the women decided it was time to change their name. In 1929, focusing on what they now were and what they had always planned to be, they renamed themselves the Women's Golf Association of Massachusetts (WGAM). With a goal of giving the women of their state the most golf possible and showing the nation they were the best, they moved into the 1930's renamed, better organized, and ready to keep on growing.

The main business of that first meeting of the WGAM was to accept and put into play the Osgood Memorial Cup, presented by Louisa Wells in honor of Fanny Osgood, who had passed away that spring. The Cup honored the low net qualifier in the Association Championship in memory of Osgood's wit and great golf game. All there were sad that Fanny wasn't present to see her true dream of a large, stable statewide association realized. Her Cup remains one of the most coveted wins each WGAM season. The Townshend Cup, given by Fanny's sister, Mrs. Hannah Townshend, was donated as the trophy for a two-day medal tournament started in 1930.

❧❧

Margaret and Harriot Curtis were determined and when the Curtis sisters set their sights on something, nothing was going to hold them back. In the late 1920's and early 1930's, they wanted international competition for women golfers. In late 1927, as a way to spur the USGA into action on the issue, the Curtis sisters donated a cup to be played for in international matches. "Our hope is we as an organization will get back to this enterprise and push it to the utmost," Margaret Curtis said. That same day, an "anonymous" donation of

> **"Steel shafted clubs will not be barred from any of the association tournaments or matches."**
>
> —*1923 WGAB Handbook*

$5,000 arrived at the WGAM offices earmarked to help defray the cost of sending a team of 10 women across the ocean to compete. Few doubt the Curtis sisters were the donors. Weeks later, the WGAM voted to back that donation with $6,000 of their own to help launch the Curtis Cup competition. Meeting notes reflect their desire for this to be a reality. "The WGAM records itself as heartily in favor of the establishment of international team matches for women golfers and pledges itself to raise for this purpose $6,000." As 1930 began, the USGA had only given a non-financial stamp of approval to the matches. While the USGA helped fund the men inter-

FASHION STATEMENT

The floor-length skirts of the early 1900's had given way to shorter, more tailored skirts in the 1930's and the women found them much more conducive to golf. Still, the attire worn on the links seems silly at best in today's world of made-for-sport wear. Patty Berg tried to shake things up at the 42nd U.S. Women's Amateur Championship by wearing oil-skinned pants, but while women in golf circles everywhere talked about the daring move, few if any followed suit.

nationally, the women were told to find a way on their own. The Curtis sisters wouldn't give up on that.

Margaret Curtis took a major step that spring of 1930 in her lifelong quest to develop good golfers when she wrote to the MGA asking help getting in touch with local golf professionals to secure the names of young girls for a possible junior championship. Curtis knew the future of the game depended on getting girls playing at a young age. Through her efforts, the first Junior Girls' Championship was set for June 30-July 3 of that year at Oakley Country Club. The first junior event drew 10 entrants, with Miss Dorothy Hunter winning. In a foreshadowing of things to come, she went on that year to win the first Townshend Cup as well, proving Curtis' point: good junior events will feed future golfers into the adult events. Indeed, Dorothy Hunter (Whittemore Beard) eventually became a four-time winner of the Association Championship.

As always, the women were well aware of the goings on in the world around them. Much of the nation and Boston were crippled by the stock market crash of 1929 and the depression was sinking deeper and deeper. Mindful of that, the Board voted to donate $200 of their tournament funds to the Unemployment Relief Fund in Boston and another $200 to the Red Cross. They also sent a check for $50 — quite a sum in that day — to Mr. D. J. McGuinness of the *Boston Globe*. McGuinness had long covered women's golf for the *Globe*, but that year lost his foot in an accident. The women felt it their place to help him out.

By 1932 the depression was hitting full force, but the women noted that "despite present conditions," their membership held steady at 77 member clubs,

COURSE MANAGEMENT 101

In the summer of 1935, the now-famed Patty Berg was playing in what was only her third tournament match when, on the 9th hole, she sliced a ball over a pond. Her ball hit a lily pad and skimmed across a number of other pads, landing on the bank of the pond in good position for the green. The gallery was amazed — just two weeks before Bobby Jones had hit that same lily pad with the same result. Berg won that match, but was defeated the next day by the WGAM's very own Glenna Collett in the finals, proving the point: you can beat Mother Nature, but not a WGAM trained golfer.

with only one resignation. That tide was soon to change. One year later, clubs and members began dropping out. "This year when down seems to be the only direction the world makes use of ... ," association Secretary Jeanette Stanwood wrote in her annual report, "the remaining members played on, as the press took note." While the men are just getting around to polishing their clubs and refurbishing their lockers, the women folk have been at it for weeks. You can call golf an old man's game or a young man's sport, but you cannot deny that when women take it up, it becomes a very serious matter," the *Transcript* newspaper gushed. "Victory and defeat are accepted with grace, but the outcome is seldom taken lightly."

In 1932, in an effort to attract more golfers, the WGAM opened up the spring Team Matches to non-handi-

capped players. "This brought out not only the grandmothers and granddaughters, but the aunts and cousins as well," said Stanwood. The spring featured many nine-hole scores above 80, and many a lost ball. But the women chalked it up to experience, and noted their original goal had actually been reached: more women had been exposed to golf. Who knew, they agreed? There could be a future champion among those who scored so high.

Equipment was improving as well, and many women now wielded steel-shafted clubs and a new ball with a rubber wound core. Still, the ladies agreed, golf was a game not easily dominated. "There is a new ball, to be sure, but it doesn't seem to make much of a difference, since the slicers still slice and the hookers still hook," an annual report noted.

By the mid 1930's, the junior events required three flights, the Association Championship was watched by hundreds and the spring team program was considering four teams per club. As the depression broke, clubs began to join again and numbers soared once more. So, too, did the public curiosity about women's golf. In 1935 The Country Club of New Bedford wrote the WGAM asking them to send down "four outstanding women golfers for an exhibition day." They did so, squeezing it into what was now a crowded calendar of women's golf events each season. They remained true to that original goal of good golf and plenty of it, keeping in mind that in golf, "good" is relative. "We hope we will be successful in planning an abundant schedule with plenty of delightful tortures for those of us

who will hook and those of us who will slice throughout the coming season," Stanwood said.

With another new influx of members, the WGAM continued its plea for knowledge of rules. "On behalf of the new chairman, I do earnestly implore you to learn to read!" the new rules chairman Arlene Kelley said as she handed out fresh rules books to members at a meeting. The newer players were getting younger too. Such events as the Junior-Senior Scotch, held for the first time in 1936, gave young and perhaps less confident golfers a chance to feel good out on the course and get some pointers at the same time. "Scared juniors found it very comforting to share their responsibilities with their senior partners and such a delightful time was had by all, the tournament will

Alice and Lucille Belanger. Alice Belanger was Junior State Champion in 1936-38.

be repeated," the WGAM notes on the event read.

Some other juniors were about to benefit from the WGAM as well. On Nov. 12, 1936, the Executive Committee met to accept a financial bonus. Bond money they had put up to help start the Eastern Women's Golf Association had matured, and $166 had fallen into their hands. Harriot Curtis proposed creating a "Caddie Educational Fund," to help boy caddies go to technical schools in

Dorothy Beard

> **"We feared the finals would be a question of survival of the hottest, not the fittest,"**
>
> *—Comment on the 1934 Association Championship, played in 100-plus degree weather.*

their area. The committee approved her proposal, and many caddies were helped along into careers through the years.

As the 1930's wound down, the women found the men were still hesitant to give them control on the course and off. The USGA wrote to the WGAM in the summer of 1937 saying any appointments to the USGA Women's Committee rested with them, an all-male group, and not with groups like the WGAM. Disappointed but not dissuaded, the WGAM sent along a list of suggested appointees, hoping one of their own would end up on the committee.

With her junior program growing to the point of needing a junior-junior division tournament, Margaret Curtis decided to set her sights on another age group and began a tour of colleges to stimulate golf for women there as well. She hoped to get women playing and

get schools to form teams. She did things in a simple, smart way. To stimulate junior play, she placed junior clubs in junior bags at golf courses throughout the state. For a returnable $10 deposit, anyone could use them.

The decade closed with a hopeful message for marriage and golf. For the first time since its beginning, the Club Pairs Mixed Foursome Championship was won by a married couple, Mr. and Mrs. Warren Beard (nee Dorothy Hunter). While those who'd jokingly called the event the "Divorce Open," cheered the possibility of a couple actually playing golf well together, the women secretly knew it was the female in the twosome who carried them. That year Dorothy had won the State Association Championship, the Eastern Championship, the Inter-City Championship, the Townshend Cup, and the Endicott Cup. In fact, the only existing championship she didn't win was the juniors, since she was ineligible because of age. (She did, however, present the trophy to the winner, having been the first-ever Junior Champion in 1930). For her and for all the WGAM ladies, golf had become much more than a diversion. There were champions in their midst. And they knew the men knew that as well. With players like Beard, the standard could not get much higher, it seemed. But it would.

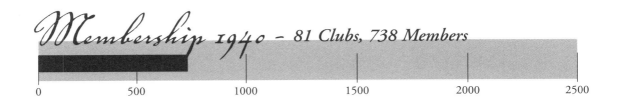

Membership 1940 – 81 Clubs, 738 Members

| 0 | 500 | 1000 | 1500 | 2000 | 2500 |

World War II

"We learned many things in 1942. It was fun sharing our cars to save gas and we gained new respect and sympathy for caddies when they (were) not available and we had to carry our own bags. I think we might say of this season that our many problems made us appreciate golf as never before."

Celia R. Turner, WGAM Secretary, 1944

No one could say WGAM women took golf too seriously. The way they welcomed the 40's was proof. Called the "Cavalcade of Ourselves," the special spring meeting at the Women's City Club on Beacon Street in Boston on April 1, 1940 was a mixture of spoof, comedy and actual Association business.

Women's Golf Association of Massachusetts

•

Indoor Spring Meeting
CAVALCADE OF OURSELVES
One-half serious and One-half foolish

•

A talking movie of how each shot should be played by
Jimmy Thompson   Harry Cooper
Lawson Little   Horton Smith
Bobby Jones

Mrs. W. Stanley Parker will show us how we have come along.

•

A Rogue's Gallery from some of the Boston newspapers.

•

Tea

Monday, April 1, 1940
at 3:00 P. M.

•

Women's City Club, 40 Beacon Street
50 Cents Admission

The point of the meeting was to stimulate interest in golf, and the program certainly caught and held the attention of everyone there. They showed an old-fashioned "talking movie" with Bobby Jones and Horton Smith demonstrating how each shot was played, and displayed a "rogue's gallery" of newspaper accounts of WGAM events. "We laughed harder than most thought was possible," one meeting note exclaimed.

Such innocent levity was to be short-lived. Across the ocean, bombs were falling and casualties building as Hitler progressed in his march across Europe. In the summer of 1939 both Britain and France had declared war on Germany. While the WGAM women were insulated from the building confrontation in their world of comfort and golf, they chose to face it head on, even before their own countrymen were affected.

Of course it was the Curtis sisters who spurred the organization to become involved. Appalled at the suffering of their friends in the Ladies' Golf Union in England, Margaret and Miss Harriot convinced the WGAM to raise money to purchase a mobile kitchen for the British Relief Fund. Germany, in an attempt to take Britain, was trying to

starve out the troops and civilians. With a special flag tournament, donations at all WGAM events and personal contributions, $1,528 — an astronomical amount in 1941 — was raised by late spring. The kitchen was delivered with an inscription: "As a tribute to the Ladies' Golf Union from the Women's Golf Association of Massachusetts USA." It was an apt gift and most appreciated. With the balance of funds, the women also were able to purchase seven hospital beds with linens for England, sending them over at a time when the vast majority of Americans were against going to war.

In January of 1941, the United States could no longer remain neutral and committed $7 billion to their Allies in the Lend-Lease Act. It was President Roosevelt's hope that money would fight the war rather than men. On December 7, 1941, the WGAM and the rest of the country realized that the disturbance overseas was going to affect more than their European counterparts. Pearl Harbor was bombed that morning, and within hours, the nation was officially at war. The women of the WGAM met three days later on the morning of December 10 for their annual meeting. The notes of that meeting read, "It is

The WGAM mobile kitchen for the British Relief Fund

agreed to plan our 1942 golf schedule as usual but with the understanding that some events might have to be cancelled or altered as war conditions make it advisable."

In fact, that meeting was far from somber and was more like a well-staged drama. Knowing it was Margaret Curtis' last meeting as President since she had announced her intention to step down months before, the membership came ready to honor this great woman and golfer. The meeting was to begin at 11 a.m. Margaret, always punctual, was nowhere to be found at that time. The minutes ticked by and the women filled the room with small talk. As the quarter hours passed, they began to look nervously at the clock. Finally, just past 11:40 a.m., the Association Vice President, Mrs. John Amory, rose and called the meeting to order. She calmly read the minutes while the women in the room wondered what could have happened to their outgoing president. As Amory read on and the attendants quietly listened, the Brae Burn club-

house door suddenly swung open with a rattle. All heads turned to look and at once, Curtis appeared, sashaying into the room dressed from head to toe in the very Gay 90's outfit she'd worn to win her first-ever golf championship. Her antique clubs slung over her shoulder, she took over the meeting, never mentioning her attire. It was a moment remembered for decades and, in true Margaret Curtis style, a great way to retire.

※—※

The WGAM Board held fast to their desire to play on through the escalating war, but as 1942 ticked on, it became apparent that this would be impossible. By the end of that year, a full 12 million American men and women would be on active duty in Europe and the Pacific. Everyone was touched by the turmoil — brothers, sisters, husbands, sons, daughters, friends, and neighbors were fighting overseas or worse, were lost to the effort. In a nation where women's roles had always been at home, women were now being called to work in the massive

restructuring of industry toward fueling a war. In Massachusetts, as across the country, gas and food rationing was in full force and everything, everything revolved around the war.

The WGAM members were left with a strange quandary: they felt deeply for the war effort and wanted to do all they could, but with so many men away at war, the golf course fairways, so crowded recently, were wide open and beckoned temptingly.

Dramatic adjustments were required. First, the Board decided that all Association prizes were to be War Bonds or Defense Stamps. Then, all major events, from the Griscom Cup to the Endicott Cup and Tri-State Matches to the Association Championship, were cancelled. Fifteen clubs actually dropped out of the Association. At a meeting to review the situation, Margaret Curtis rose and spoke with conviction. "We should use our imagination and all our resources to keep golf going during these times," she said. The officers decided to put into place more lenient

> **"We must give our members the opportunity to enjoy, to a limited extent at least, the comradeship of golf."**
> — *Margaret Curtis, 1942*

handicap rules for wartime (for instance, scores made on courses where preferred lies were in effect were allowed to be used for computing the handicap if no other scores were available), thus allowing new players and those not able to play as often to compete. They also

Deborah Verry

current President, Deborah Verry, a member of the Waves branch of the Naval Reserves, was called overseas to duty on Dec. 22, 1942. She sent a letter of regret to the Association offering her resignation. The Board would have nothing of it, and voted to keep her as President and appoint Dorothy (Hunter Whittemore) Beard as Acting President. Verry served in the Waves until the end of the war and then went on to join the CIA in Washington. She was kept on as President until her term concluded at the end of 1943.

Just when they doubted their contribution to the war was enough, the WGAM received word in June that a Massachusetts soldier fighting in Ipswich District, one of the most blitzed parts of the British Isles, had seen their effort. As gunfire and explosives filled the air around him, he approached a mobile kitchen for a bite to eat. As he tried to choke down some food in that horrible place, the inscription on the kitchen unit caught his eye. He smiled broadly. The golfing gals back home were thinking of him. Dinner never tasted better. In September of 1943, with the Association Championship cancelled, a Red Cross Tournament was held instead, raising $151 to continue the WGAM's efforts to help their nation.

At the 1943 annual meeting, the attending members made a personal sacrifice, each donating two impossible-to-get golf balls. The collection was boxed, stamped and sent off to Sgt. Frank Strafaci, an amateur golf teacher stationed with troops in the South Pacific. Strafaci was using golf as a way for soldiers to relieve stress. With the rationing on rubber and plastic all but halting golf ball produc-

tion, it was hard for the WGAM members to share from their dwindling supplies. Still, one has to think it must have bettered the donors' games. The pressure of knowing fewer balls existed must have strengthened their determination not to lose any with wayward drives or with careless approach shots over water hazards.

Caddies were hard, if not impossible, to find. For decades the women had been coddled by always having their clubs carried. Now they were forced to sling them over their shoulders and tote them along. Tournament prizes were cut nearly in half as a way to pinch pennies in the lean times as well.

With their shorter skirts and more comfortable clothing designed to accommodate working women, and with more tee times available at area courses, the WGAM members saw their games improve. A new, determined breed of female golfer was evolving.

By the end of 1944 the WGAM and the nation were beginning to see the light at the end of the tunnel. Made hopeful by the Allies' success at Normandy and by the Battle of the Bulge that winter, the Board voted, if hesitantly, to look toward a war-free future. With a show-of-hands vote, they agreed to return to normal team play

"If worst comes to worst, we will all be playing on snowshoes and hitting a little red ball to something reminiscent of a green."

— *Item on weather in the 1948 Member Newsletter*

decided to hold tournaments to benefit the war effort, and to continue supporting the troops. Team matches were adjusted to allow for train travel and later starts since gas was so hard to obtain. In a letter to members in the fall of 1943, the Association declared their regular golf games good for the war effort. The letter reminded members, "It is our patriotic duty to keep in shape!"

The war also forced the Association to do something it had never done before: appoint an acting President. The

that spring "if conditions warrant." On April 30, Hitler committed suicide in his Berlin bunker. In August, the atom bombs fell and by Fall, the war that had changed everything was over.

But the change was forever. Women had learned to see themselves as capable contributors, had stepped out of their long skirts and corsets, and would never again be content in the shadows of industry.

➶-❧

Slowly, clubs rejoined the WGAM. In 1946, the Tri-State competition, team matches, and all other championship events resumed. While the Board had made concessions for the disruptions of the war years, they knew they had to get back to the real rules and real object of the game. Anyone who had been unable to play in those years was granted a temporary handicap good through May 28 for team play. They stuck to the deadline, insisting all handicaps were required to be in place after that date. With regret, they dropped 95 players who did not get new handicaps in on time. Like the nation they lived in, they'd come out of the war stronger and more confident. "The Association is resuming a pre-war schedule and this means a pre-war adherence to golf rules and handicapping," they stated in early 1946. Just to make sure everyone understood things were back to normal, a copy of the 1946 rules book was mailed to every member with a note reminding them to study up.

It was clear the war years had forged a newer, stronger golfer. Nancy Black

Gene O'Neil (McAuliffe)

was one, winning her first Association Championship the summer of 1946 at Charles River Country Club. Following in the footsteps of Margaret Curtis, she did it with flourish, winning it all on the 19th hole. Black, destined to be one of the most winning WGAM members, had learned to play golf from her father, who was a well-respected doctor. Black adopted her father's traditional swing which produced an overspin with lots of roll. She was, from the start, a fierce competitor with an amazing all around game. When she took to the course, she intended to win..period. And if she needed a good chip, putt or drive, she always had it there in her bag. With this first championship win, she sent that message loud and clear.

Players of all ages were eager to get back to golf after the years of going without. The junior tournament that August was

proof of that, and also showcased the talented younger women the WGAM was bringing along. Played at South Shore Country Club on August 27-30, the event was cut down to nine holes on the final day because of torrential rain, hazardous winds and chilly temperatures. "Defying torrential rains, 18-year-old Ann Cosgrove (Boros) of Marshfield slopped her way over flooded fairways and soggy greens," one newspaper report said. Gene O'Neil (McAuliffe) was the winner though, beating Cosgrove by overcoming a three-hole deficit. By the way, the junior boys, slated to play the same day, postponed until better weather. The hardy WGAM golfers were back and on their heels were juniors like Cosgrove, Pippy Rooney and O'Neil, destined to become champions.

➶-❧

More and more women were flocking to the sport. In 1946 alone, an amazing 147 new golfers applied for WGAM handicaps. A new publication, "Lady Golfer," premiered to an ever-growing audience. And for those in the game from the start, a new WGAM championship debuted. The Senior Championship, with a cup donated by the Curtis sisters, was played October 10 at Brae Burn and was won by Mrs. Christopher Haig of Winthrop with a 95. In the fall of 1947, the *Boston Herald*, bowing to the constant demands of the WGAM, agreed to begin printing women's golf news. Perhaps the best sign of all that women golfers were getting better and better came at the 1947 annual meeting: the Hole-in-One award debuted. Five women were honored that first year. And while they would have liked to have been awarded a sleeve of golf balls, all the awards that year were gift certificates instead. Golf balls, one of the biggest casualties of the war, were still impossible to find. Similarly, caddies remained scarce, with many young men not yet home from the war or back and taking advantage of GI Bill school benefits. At the end of the meeting, Mrs. Theo Hunting rose and read a poem she had composed.

> "Four near golf-less years have come
>   and gone
> But we're back at the game again.
> Matches, tournaments, gripes and all
> No wonder Eleanor is so thin!
>
> Though there's been no meat, no
>   gasoline
> We've lugged our clubs with ease.
> But oh for the day when we can say
> Take the pin, caddy, please."

In the spring of 1948, the number of members enrolled in team match play grew to 300, a huge number not only in terms of participation, but also in terms of the organization required. At the helm of that massive effort was Eleanor LaBonte, the unassuming, kind-hearted master of the WGAM. On the payroll since 1937, LaBonte's official title was Executive Secretary, but more often, members referred to her as "general." LaBonte was not a jovial woman, and while she was warm and caring to all who knew her, her first impression could be summed up in two words: in charge.

Clearly someone had to be. The Association was growing in ways never imagined. The finances were more complicated, handicaps numbered near a thousand, and golf rounds overseen by the WGAM were well into the thousands. Yet LaBonte had command of it all. "She could tell you your handicap if you just asked her," remembered Pippy Rooney O'Connor. "And no one ever

*Left to Right: Dolly Sullivan, Nancy Black and Edith N. Baker
1947 WGAM Association Championship at Belmont*

questioned her. She really knew the WGAM."

Those huge numbers, however, did not breed a climate of strangers. In fact, many of the WGAM members were longtime friends or even family. A case in point was the 1948 Association Championship, pitting Florence McClusky of Worcester Country Club against her aunt, Julie Norby of Wachusett Country Club, medalist at that tournament. Floss McClusky won 6 and 5 in the quarterfinals and went on to win the Championship, giving Norby the consolation at least of losing to the winner when the subject came up at the family holiday table. But the big talk was probably still McClusky's final match against Laddie Homer of Brae Burn. On the 19th hole, Homer had put the ball on the green, just 25 feet from the hole. McClusky hit her second shot short and had a 45-foot chip. She chipped in, thrilling the crowd. Homer still had a chance to halve the hole, and

stepped up to her putt, focused and stroked the ball. She hit it dead on, but too short, with the ball stopping just six inches from the hole. Floss McClusky had won the first of her five WGAM Championships.

The decade closed with the war a painful but receding memory. Golf balls were getting easier to find and the caddies were back. The women of the WGAM had weathered it all, and done so with class, supporting their troops and yet preserving their Association and the game they loved. At the close of the decade, their numbers totaled 72 clubs and 856 members, the highest ever. The real growth was yet to come. But none of it would have been possible without the strange juxtaposition of a war, women left to their own devices and wide-open fairways. For that, women's golf owes history a thank you.

Birth of the Spring Team Competition

It had started as a way for women to make golfing acquaintances and to learn to compete. The idea proved to be very successful and perennially popular. For the first three years there were six matches between several competing clubs. To accommodate more clubs, the format was changed in 1903 to individual stroke play on one day in May, and any player from the member clubs could participate. The scoring was changed to one point for attendance, one point for the match, and one point for the team win. In 1915 four regional divisions were established and the format was returned to match play on five days in May. In the fall of 1946, the WGAM introduced a new way of playing spring team matches, to debut in the spring of 1947. Called the "Cup Series," the program was designed to allow another 100 or more women to play in the spring matches. The club teams would be seeded by handicap, promising close, competitive play and providing an easy way for the program to grow.

For the thirty-two years before this change there were four divisions: Northern, Western, Southern and The Country Club (The Country Club had its own team). Beginning in 1947, the matches would be divided into as many "cups" as were needed. The only hitch was that each club had to field five players who met the handicap restrictions. The Board knew this would be difficult for some clubs, but looked at it as an incentive for more women players to get handicaps and to work to lower their scores. Members like Eleanor Allen and Edith Baker donated trophies for specific cups. In that first year of the Cup Series, 270 women played on 54 teams, which were seeded into 9 cups. The program has continued to grow through the years and remains the backbone of the WGAM competitive schedule. In the Spring of 2000, 855 women played on 171 teams, which were seeded into 29 Cups. Clearly, Spring Team matches remain a wonderful way to make golfing acquaintances, play new courses, hone competitive skills, and solidify team camaraderie.

Membership 1950 – 73 Clubs, 952 Members

| 0 | 500 | 1000 | 1500 | 2000 | 2500 |

Mid-Century

"Sure it's fun to win, but someone has to lose too. This trend of making games practically a business is growing in all sports in this country. I suppose this is the result of professional playing of all games. To have it spread to amateurs is, in my thinking, deplorable. We must fight it."

—- May Jackson, President, 1948

Half a century had passed. Although they had fifty years of experience building their sport, the WGAM women knew that they had much more work ahead of them. More and more women were rushing to get their first handicap. The call for competition was now louder and being answered in new and creative ways. Mildred Prunaret and Carol Cooney (Burns) had won the reinstated Senior-Junior Tournament the autumn before. In 1950 Edith Baker donated a prize - a special gold bracelet - with the request that a tournament of "a very popular kind," be held, one that would take place in the summer and at a nice vacation spot to make working women and students happy. That same year Grace Keyes donated the Keyes Cup for a WGAM stroke-play championship.

The WGAM Board knew a celebration was called for. The 50th anniversary was marked with a free tournament

"Wishing you good golf for the next 50 years!"

—Card to the WGAM from Joyce H Bailey, member

at Oakley Country Club that unfortunately had to be held in sleet and rain. *Boston Transcript* reporter A. Linde Fowler pointed out, "The weather cooperated by being raw and cold so that the 134 players could prove their stamina was no less than those ladies who teed off 50 years ago." Prevailing to win the event were Nancy Black and Florence McClusky.

A 50th Anniversary tea was held at The Country Club in Brookline and was highlighted by the appearance of Margaret and Harriot Curtis and Grace Keyes in circa 1900 clothing. Usually reserved Miss Harriot approached the center of the room, teed up a ball, pulled out a club and sent the ball soaring — right through a closed window of the clubhouse and out onto the fairway, leaving fragments of shattered

Grace Keyes (left), and Harriot Curtis at the 50th anniversary of the founding of the Women's Golf Association.

— The Boston Globe - March 21, 1950

glass behind. In true fellow-competitor form, Keyes spotted the ball for her all the way. The ball Harriot hit, by the way, was a Gutta Percha. Celebration

The South Shore Women's Golf League (1952) - Left to right, front row: Mary Gleason, Betty Cave, Priscilla Bailey, Edith Baker, Helen Howard. Back row: Pippy Rooney, Dolly Sullivan, Kathleen Heffernan, Jeanne Colby, Pat Murray.

aside, 1950 was a time of huge change for women golfers. Before the war, women's presence had been tolerated on men's golf courses as a nice way to fill the fairways on slower days. However, in the post-war boom, as more men and more women took up the sport, the attitudes began to change. Gone were the depression days when clubs were desperate for new members. There was instead the new era of waiting lists, booked tee times and members-come-first policies. The ladies faced a dilemma: they needed to schedule more tournaments and matches to satisfy their growing ranks, but clubs were more and more reluctant to share their courses.

When the clubs did agree to host events, they usually found them to be exciting and worthy of great publicity. The 1951 Association Championship at Charles River Country Club certainly

was a case in point. This major tournament had three past champions in the field and all were looking for a repeat performance. Florence McClusky, Ruth Woodward, and Nancy Black were each looking for another big win. The press gave the event the most publicity of any WGAM event to that day. The entire golf population, it seemed, was looking on. Even Patty Berg was in the gallery to watch. No one was disappointed by the show.

The excitement began in the first match, with Mrs. Albert Buffman of Winchester upsetting the medalist Mrs. Willard Howard in a 24-hole marathon, the longest WGAM tournament match to date. In the end it was Laddie Homer who went on to win it all. The press was taken with her aggressive style. "Mrs. Homer putts with her hands apart very much like Ty Cobb's batting style," the

Boston Herald noted. The entire event had featured close matches and talented players.

Where did such a large group of top players come from? The WGAM now had a large pool to draw from. In the spring team matches of 1953, 84 teams were vying for 14 cups. That meant a total of 528 players were part of the spring team program. In June the membership list topped 1,000.

By 1953 the WGAM knew the boom was far from over. Faced with so many new members and so many more tournaments, the Board called upon member Clarissa "Cris" Eaton to serve as rules chairman and impose strict standards. In a memo, Eaton humorously told how tough her job was. "It is helpful, though not always possible, to have a member of the Rules Committee, the USGA, even the Supreme Court available for final interpretation." Her committee even voted to end the prac-

> **"If I, in some small way, have helped you increase your interest in golf, I am well rewarded."**
>
> *— Mildred Prunaret,*
>
> *stepping down as president in 1951.*

tice of free coffee and doughnuts before tee-off in order to decrease delays in starting times.

The WGAM was desperate for club cooperation. With a large calendar of events, they needed clubs to give them time and a place to play their game. Invitations were sent out to club and league chairwomen for a first-ever meeting of the minds at the home of

Pippy Rooney

WGAM member Helen (Mrs. Thomas) Oleson. The WGAM's motive was simple: they needed to befriend those who held power at individual clubs if they were to get those clubs to support the WGAM program. January 14, 1954, the morning of the first ever Chairmen's meeting, dawned disastrous. A blanket of snow covered the ground and more snow was accumulating fast. It was bitter cold and blowing like crazy. Oleson looked out her Wellesley Hills window and wondered how they'd ever get the women to feel comfortable after dragging them through such a storm.

Rather than cancel, she took to the kitchen to bake fresh doughnuts and then built a crackling fire in her massive fireplace. The petite blonde arranged the perfect setting. The chairwomen felt welcome and cared for. Bonds were formed and the WGAM hoped more

clubs would come on board to host tournaments.

Once the snow melted, it was 23-year old Pippy Rooney, with her short-cropped hair and broad smile, who was again grabbing headlines and trophies. The summer before she'd made changes to her swing. The result? She won the Baker, the Keyes Cup and was medalist in the Association Championship. As much as her

GREATER BOSTON IS UNDERSTANDABLY PROUD OF SOME OF THE MOST PULCHRITUDINOUS SPORTS CHAMPIONS IN THE NATION

Theodora Pippy ROONEY, MASSACHUSETTS WOMEN'S GOLF CHAMPION, HAILS FROM JAMAICA PLAIN

swing was reported on, so too was her fashion sense. Pippy had a way of choosing outfits that made the press take note. One news report referred to her "purple people eater pants," and another talked of her bright blouse. Like Rooney, more and more women were taking fashion risks on the course, something the Association felt obligated to police. After their counterparts in Connecticut ruled against shorts worn at their events, the WGAM voted that

"Shorts must be knee length if worn at Association events." Reading that new ruling at the annual meeting, Association secretary Joyce Bailey hinted at most women's feeling about it by introducing it as "on the more amusing side."

While the press seemed set on reporting the fashion trends of the Association, there was plenty of golf to talk about too. By 1954, Rooney wasn't the only young star. The young woman the press called "a petite precisionist from Plymouth," 18-year-old Joanne Goodwin, beat the powerful Nancy Black in the final match of the Championship. Goodwin, who had graduated from high school just a week before, had begged a ride from the South Shore to the Championship with Black. A month later, Goodwin won the last junior crown for which she would be eligible.

That wasn't the only place the young were taking over. Sixteen-year old Betty Dargie and 15-year old James "Jay" Dolan III of Hillcrest won the popular Stone Cup Club Pairs event later that summer. Goodwin won the Endicott Cup that fall. The stronger junior program was paying off and more and more young women were growing into full-scale WGAM members.

But rules were still being broken. Now President, Cris Eaton held tightly

"I wanted to make sure I was up near the water fountain, so I aimed my tee shot well to the right. It was stifling hot and I was looking forward to a drink."

— *Pippy Rooney on a tournament shot she used showing unique course management.*

Joanne Goodwin

to her belief in rules and read aloud a USGA letter on the topic at the 1955 annual meeting. "Cheating can happen wherever there is a motive other than the play for the game's sake. Golf is being used for ulterior purposes in some quarters." She pointed to the practice of some in keeping high handicaps, using "soft" local rules with no justification, winking at violations of rules of amateur status and what she called the "over-commercialization" of the game, and read more of the letter. "All do violence to the concept that golf is a game of sportsmanship and should be an end in itself." She beseeched her fellow golfers to set an example in sportsmanship not only for their newest members, but also for the sport as a whole. Now that the WGAM was one of the strongest and largest women's golf groups in the nation, it was their obligation, Eaton said.

Nationally, the WGAM was definitely recognized as a power. Mildred Prunaret was becoming one of the best-known proponents for women's golf in the nation. She traveled to Europe and across the country for meetings on women's golf, helping organize the sport around the world. May Jackson, a softer-spoken member and former president with a good game of her own, was known as a champion of rules, etiquette and proper play. And the names Keyes, Eaton, Baker and Allen were becoming legendary in women's golf circles.

❧❧

The war was long over but Margaret Curtis hadn't forgotten those who had suffered its miseries. In 1955, she was busy putting together her "Swing Clubs," which were driving ranges at Veteran's Hospitals where volunteers would teach vets to play golf as a way to relieve stress. She was now 71 years old and less competitive; however, she and her sister were still revered by the WGAM. At the 1954 Annual Meeting,

"Golf is still the greatest game of all in my opinion. You don't have to play well to enjoy it."

— Margaret Curtis, 1959, after scoring a 108 at Marshfield.

Margaret Curtis was presented with the Curtis Bowl, a sterling trophy for a new tournament to be played in honor of the two grand ladies of golf. Set up as foursomes, an alternate shot event, the Curtis Bowl remains one of the most popular annual tournaments on the WGAM schedule. Margaret, for the first time in most memories, was left speechless. After standing, stunned, for a full minute, she found her voice and got back to business, asking for help at her Swing Clubs, urging more work on the junior program and throwing in a few historic anecdotes. She also invited anyone who was to play in the first Curtis Bowl tournament back to her home for fish chowder after the event. As usual, Margaret Curtis found a way to accept a

MORE OOPS MOMENTS

During the first round of team matches in May of 1953, Betty Scholl of Charles River Country Club made a hole-in-one on the fourth hole of that course. In the excitement, her opponent, Mrs. Francis Turner of Weston forgot to play the hole, and, as the media noted, "thereby passed up a chance to make an ace on her own account."

gift and give something back in return.

Margaret was rewarded with a great round in the 1956 season opener - a special event at Woodland Golf Club. At 72 years old, she shot a 93 (net 81), taking third net honors while playing in a heavy housedress. Not the least upset by the over-90 score, she understood her personal victory like the true champion she was. "The round was worthwhile," she said afterward. "I learn something new about golf every time I play."

She also took great pride in another coveted victory that year, when the WGAM Griscom Cup Team brought home the cup for the first time since 1936, proof that the junior program, expanded spring teams competition and the hard work she had done all those years was paying off. Massachusetts won 14-7 over New York at Charles River Country Club. Philadelphia didn't play that year. One reason Massachusetts beat the powerful New York team: like the veteran Nancy Black, young Joanne Goodwin prevailed to take all three Nassau points in her match.

The most talked-about match of 1956 came in June when, for the first time, Pippy Rooney faced off against Joanne Goodwin in the finals of the Association Championship at Salem Country Club. The two had never met head-to-head, never mind in the final of such an important event, and the press had a field day with that. "Dream Clash!" one headline declared. "Duelists at 18 paces," another paper called the two. And just to make sure everyone understood the excitement and importance of the event, Pippy's friend Ellen Gery buzzed the course in a Piper Cub.

The two kept the huge gallery guessing, halving the front nine, as both shot 39. But in the end, Goodwin's precision prevailed, 4 and 3. "Joanne hit the ball so straight the next ball she loses is like-

3rd Annual Senior-Junior Tournament (1954)

ly to be her first," the *Herald* reported.

Cris Eaton herself weighed in on Goodwin's accomplishments. "Her golf game is perhaps not spectacular — unless one calls steadiness, accuracy, perfect timing and grooving spectacular. But it certainly is a pleasure to watch her play." And, said Eaton, the most important thing about Goodwin was her firm grasp of what the game, and

the WGAM, is all about. "She is modest, reserved and willing to play with hackers and still able to make them feel at ease."

The publicity, the high level of competition, the vision of more women on the course was pushing the number of female golfers even higher. A study by the USGA in 1957 found that 375,000 women had taken up golf in America in

Joanne Goodwin and Barbara McIntyre

nent because the gallery was loud, and then went on to lose the match one down. To Curtis, that was the ultimate act of a champion. In her mind, doing the right thing was always much more important than winning.

By late 1958 the WGAM was getting more publicity, but the press was patronizing at times, joking about moms begging dads to baby-sit so they could play, poking fun at fashion and even calling the Eleanor Allen Bowl winners "a pair of comely brunettes." It was clear the press was willing to cover women golfers, but not with the same serious note given to their male counter-parts.

If the press wasn't serious about women's play, it didn't affect the effort of the competitors or the spirit of the galleries. In the Association Championship second round in 1958, Dolly Sullivan celebrated her 44th birthday by overcoming a four-hole deficit to beat defending champion Mrs. Bea Bower on the 19th hole at Worcester Country Club. As she tapped in her last putt, the gallery broke into a chorus of "Happy Birthday to You." Dolly's age provided for some fun entertainment but in the end, youth prevailed. The tournament was won by 21 year-old Goodwin and the average age of the semifinalists was just 25.

On other fairways, the less youthful were providing strong competition for one another. In the 1958 Senior Championship, Kathleen Heffernan,

the previous three years. In 1947, WGAM membership had totaled 400. In 1957, it stood at 1,450. Men were apparently beginning to understand that women did indeed make major, positive impacts on golf. To prove that, in December of 1957 at the Drake Hotel in Chicago, the USGA named Margaret Curtis the fourth winner of the Bobby Jones Award for Distinguished Sportsmanship in Golf. She was 73 at the time and unable to make the trip. She sent Mildred Prunaret in her place,

who listened with pride as Totton P. Heffelfinger described Curtis as "a great lady, a great golfer, who has through the years in every move she has made in golf shown she is one of the great sportswomen of all time." Prunaret read a letter from Curtis in which Curtis remembered what she considered Bobby Jones' greatest championship moment. As she watched, Jones gave a "missable" putt to his oppo-

> **"I really wouldn't be out here in this rain, but I promised Dolly back last winter . . ."**
>
> *Golf great Francis Ouimet on his appearance, and win in the Mixed Foursomes with his niece, Dolly Sullivan*

mother of nine children, won with an 85. And while Mrs. M.E. Philbrick, 79, didn't fare as well (128-101), she had an explanation for her score in the tournament for which she had donated the trophy. "Naturally, it would be rude of me to come out here and win my own bowl," she quipped. Another senior player, Caroline ("Girlie") Bartholomew, had an exceptional 1959 season, winning the North and South Senior Championship (a national event), the Brae Burn Club Championship, the Dedham Country and Polo Club Championship, and the WGAM Senior Championship. She was runner up in the Association Championship to boot. With the total clubs associating themselves with the WGAM now at 100, there was plenty of talent across the spectrum of ages.

The decade was a boon for all but particularly for Margaret Curtis. At the last annual meeting of the 1950's she rose and announced, "My hobby has been most rewarding," then handed out the 26 golf balls she'd found in the rough and out of bounds at 7:15 that morning. Several fortunate members still cherish the balls they were given that day, autographed by Margaret herself.

Birth of the Blue Book

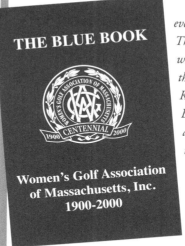

THE BLUE BOOK

Women's Golf Association of Massachusetts, Inc. 1900-2000

It comes in the mail every year and without even reading the cover, you know what to call it: The Blue Book. But where did it come from and why is it called the Blue Book? It all started with the celebration of the WGAM's 50th anniversary. Knowing it was a monumental occasion, the Board decided to try hiring a writer to produce a book on their half-century of history. Unable to find the right writer or enough historic data to pull it all together, the book instead became a more expansive version of their annual event calendar and committee listings, with added information to make it an "All you need to know" book about the WGAM. It wasn't titled the "Blue Book" then, rather just "The WGAM." The color they chose for the book was the color they'd chosen for their 50th anniversary invitations: a pleasing blue. Members enjoyed the handy pocket-sized reference so much, it was decided to put one out annually. It wasn't until the 1981 issue that it was labeled "The Blue Book", its informal nickname from the start.

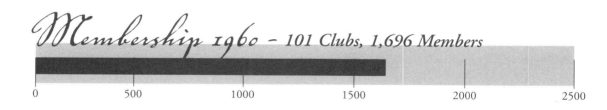

Membership 1960 – 101 Clubs, 1,696 Members

| 0 | 500 | 1000 | 1500 | 2000 | 2500 |

Coming Into Our Own
THE '60'S AND 70'S

"From the very beginning of my competitive career, the WGAM has been a part of me. The first competitive tournament I played in, at the age of thirteen, was sponsored by the WGAM. The WGAM consists of dedicated women who know and share in the spirit of the sport." —

Noreen Friel Uihlein, member of the 1978 Curtis Cup team;
three-time winner of the WGAM Association Championship (1973, 1980, 1981)

Times were good and golf mania was in full swing. Television had taken a role as primary family entertainment and each week families gathered around the set to watch Shell's Wonderful World of Golf, choosing their favorite pro, watching for swing tips and second-guessing shots. In golf, as in all sports, professional athletes were becoming celebrities.

In Massachusetts, amateur golfers still reigned supreme. Full page spreads, breathless play-by-plays that ran multiple columns, editorial cartoons and pictorials all filled the Boston sports pages, regularly featuring WGAM events and players. It was no wonder. The incredible mix of long-time players like Edith Baker and Cris Eaton and up-and-coming contenders was an elixir of golf excellence.

Led by the "Petite Precisionist from Plymouth," Joanne Goodwin, WGAM players were

Margaret and Harriot Curtis at the Curtis Cup matches in England - May 1960

showing the state, nation and world just how great women's golf could be. Joanne had been the runner-up in the 1959 USGA Women's Amateur Championship. In 1960, she was chosen to play on the United States' Curtis Cup team – the first Bay State woman named to the team since its inception in 1932.

"We were all just thrilled by it," said Pippy Rooney O'Connor, a contemporary of Goodwin's and her toughest competition at the time. If Goodwin's selection for the team wasn't exciting enough, the WGAM was further honored when Mildred Prunaret (Association President in 1950 and 1951) was chosen to be the team's Captain. Prunaret's team, which included Judy Bell, her protégé who went on to be the first female President of the USGA in the 1990's, brought home the win for

America. Boston headlines screamed the news and saluted Goodwin and Prunaret for doing the Curtis sisters proud. Although Goodwin lost her match in the Curtis Cup (one down to the British Amateur Champion, Ruth Porter), she'd made her mark as a great woman golfer. "She never knew where the rough was probably," said competitor Nancy Black of Goodwin's ability.

O'Connor, back from a summer tour playing top amateurs across the nation, was now teaching school and fighting for the right to teach golf to girls in school. Golf professionals, mostly men at the time, were staunchly opposed, fearing they'd lose clientele if girls could learn at school. And while O'Connor considered going pro, in the end, she went into the 1960's knowing she didn't belong on the touring circuit. It wasn't lack of ambition or ability, but a lifestyle choice that determined her direction.

She realized this at the time she was in Florida, staying at the fabled Breakers Hotel and playing with Babe Didrickson Zaharias. "It was the biggest thrill of my life," she said. "Babe was the best in the country, and I was paired with her. We were staying at this wonderful location and you know what? All anyone had on her mind was her own golf. That cured me. I thought there should be more to life." So Pippy chose to remain an amateur. She returned from her tour and immediately beat Flossie McClusky in the Championship.

The Massachusetts golf scene was the better for it. "Massachusetts competition was so strong because there were five or six great players who did not go to the pros," O'Connor said. Certainly the temptation was great since the women's professional tour was coming of age. Not everyone, though, thought that was best.

"Television has turned the current crop of young golfers into a flock of great imitators," said Edith Noblit Baker in the early 1960's. "Good, bad or indifferent, television has taken hold of the young golfer. And I'm not altogether sure the result isn't all bad."

Baker and others worried about the trends to flashier dress, slower play, and a focus on winning rather than sportsmanship. The WGAM, in true form, fought to preserve the integrity of the game. With the diverse membership came all sorts of style. Said one tongue-in-cheek report of the 1963 Association Championship held at Haverhill,

"There were shots, shorts, and too-short shorts at the State Women's Golf Championship Tuesday. The A-HEM line has been exceeded." Soon after, a sign was posted at WGAM events to remind women that "some shorts being worn are too short. Bermuda Length is required. Refer to Blue Book, Page 13." Still, as fashionable hemlines inched up toward the ultimate mini-skirt, and with the pros on television trying daring looks, the membership was sorely tempted.

⊹⊱

The WGAM had started out with

1962 Griscom Cup Team - Front row: (Left to right) Nancy Black, Florence McClusky, Bea Bower, Isabelle Boyden - Back row: (Left to right) Pippy Rooney, Gene McAuliffe, Nancy Thomas, Anne Nicolls, Carolyn ("Girlie") Bartholomew

member clubs clustered near Boston and with few exceptions the Association Championship had been held at clubs in the metropolitan area. Now the WGAM was strong statewide and the Board decided to hold the 1964 Association Championship on the South Shore for the first time, choosing tough and lovely Marshfield Country Club as the site. The club readied itself with all the South Shore women helping make the tournament the best ever. Then the unthinkable happened. A tornado, seldom seen in that part of the state, ripped through the course on July 4, uprooting trees, destroying greens and leaving a mess behind.

While the greenkeepers of the club worked valiantly to clean up, they had a helping hand. Cris Eaton,

driven to and from the course each day from her home by her gardener, donned garden gloves, took up her tools and helped clear the fairways for the big event. Two weeks later they were ready,

Cris Eaton

"Turn them into caddies. You can start them in the back yard in the sandbox letting them shag balls."

— *Parenting advice from Cris Eaton in 1965, then grandmother of nine and a golfer since 1909.*

though exceptional local rules were required. Preferred lies (after tee shots only) and free lifts from fallen trees (two club lengths, no nearer the hole) were necessary concessions. The WGAM had outfoxed Mother Nature and Dana

Lombard outplayed the competition to go home the winner.

Mother Nature had her way two months later though, when the threat of Hurricane Gladys canceled the Keyes Cup, slated for September 23-24. The forecast of high winds and rain led tournament officials to call it off. The hurricane never hit and more than one woman golfer, long accustomed to facing down the weather, mumbled a disappointed "told you so."

By the middle of 1965, Association membership approached the 2,000 mark, making it one of the largest and strongest women's golf groups in the nation. But a swelling membership made it no easier to find courses to host WGAM events. In New Jersey, the same was true. The women there were forced to cancel their Association Championship that year when no club would host it. The WGAM Board vowed to do their utmost to avoid such an occurrence in Massachusetts.

If the women seemed intoxicated with the successes of their growth, it could have been more than that. At the 1965 Association Championship held at The Country Club, Flossie McClusky was down two on the ninth hole to defending champion Dana Lombard when a delivery arrived. A chilled bottle of champagne was placed in her hands along with a note from her husband that read "Win, lose or draw." (He was at Worcester Country Club playing his own round.) She buckled down, pulled ahead and beat Lombard. On the 18th green, she poured the champagne into the Association Championship Cup and toasted the gallery and her victory. Lombard, no sore

Flossie McClusky quaffs champagne provided by her husband with the help of runner-up, Dana Lombard.

loser, happily rose to the occasion and helped drink the bubbly.

That was just one of the celebrations during 1965 that resulted in it being known as "The Year of the Floss." McClusky won the Association Championship for the fourth time, the Keyes Cup for the seventh, the Baker Trophy for the first, the Class A Four Ball (the Prunaret) for the first, the Curtis Bowl for the first and the Worcester Country Club Championship for the thirteenth time.

"She was the ultimate golfer. It was her life," said Nancy Black. "She had no children and a husband who adored her. Her dad was Willie Ogg, the Scottish Pro. She had plenty of time to practice and play and she was a player. She had a classic golf swing, probably one of the most beautiful swings you saw in the whole world, including the pros. If she was at the top of her game today, she'd

give any pro a run for their money."

Still, in the deep talent of the WGAM, she found competition every time.

❖❖

With almost 2,000 members, 19 cups in the Spring Team matches, and overseeing literally thousands of rounds of golf, it is remarkable that the WGAM managed its operations without the benefit of computers, fax machines or answering machines. They had one amazing weapon to attack their mounds of paperwork and endless need for management decisions. Her name was Eleanor LaBonte.

"She knew more than any of us, even if we were the president," said Nancy Black of LaBonte. "You were sent an agenda and told, 'this is what the meeting will be about.' She handed you the gavel, let you bang it, then took over. More times than not, what you decided

in the end was what she wanted in the first place. She just had a way of making that happen."

While LaBonte wasn't the gentlest of characters, her dedication to the group was unsurpassed. For years, meetings were held in her Newton Centre home, where all the WGAM files sat in her attic. ("If that house had caught fire, we'd have been in big trouble," Black quipped). Some of the women called her "The General," because when Eleanor ordered, you jumped. She did every single handicap by hand, and could tell you yours in a snap. Not that it was always accurate.

"In 1946 when I was Association Champion, my handicap went from a six to a three because she changed it," said Black. "I asked her why and she said, 'We cannot have an Association Champion who is a six!' That's just the way she was."

She was also organized, willing to put in endless hours, and while not exactly lovable, she had the best interest of the entire association in mind. As the sixties moved on, the Board began to suspect a time would come when they would need other resources. But for the time being, the good work of "The General" kept them moving along.

The year 1965 ended with both high and low notes for the WGAM. To the women's delight and for the good of all women's golf in the state, The Boston Globe hired Kitte Desmond as a golf columnist at the end of that year. Desmond would go on to write eloquently and light-heartedly of the WGAM both for the Globe and for the WGAM's annual newsletter, called "Flying Divots," for years. There is no doubt that, had she still been alive, she'd have penned these pages. No player held such a love of the game combined with a wonderful grasp of the language. But tempering the enjoyment of Kitte's new role, was the sad occurrence of Margaret Curtis' death on Christmas day. While she was not one of the six WGAB founders, she was in every mind the mother of the WGAM. To this day, she's loved and respected, idiosyncrasies and all.

❦

Within months the WGAM was to experience another major loss. The lovely, gracious Cris Eaton died that winter. Eaton, never a champion but always a staunch supporter of the WGAM and an avid golfer, was mourned deeply by the entire membership.

"She wasn't the best player, but I would say she was the most beloved member," said O'Connor. "She was extremely bright, and served as head of the school committee in Wellesley. She was a founder of the New England Women's Golf Association (NEWGA). She was a good player with a better short game. She was a great chipper and putter. And she was a lady through and through. Everything about her was first class. She was very organized and loved to be in charge, yet no one ever disliked her."

At her funeral, talk began about how much Cris loved the alternate shot format, where she could team her wonderful short game with a long-hitting partner for competitive play. Funds started to be gathered for a tournament in her memory. That next summer, the Cris Eaton Foursomes debuted at Marshfield Country Club, where she

had worked diligently to clean up after a tornado for the Association Championship. Enough money was raised to waive entry fees and all players were invited to compete for free. Of course the field filled immediately, with 175 pairs teeing off and another 100

Pat O'Brien and Flossie McClusky

pairs turned away. This annual partner event remains one of the best-loved events on the WGAM calendar.

❦

The young and the old were making news that summer of 1966. For the newer players, a Class E Championship debuted at Ponkapoag. While the press poked fun at the event ("one caddie on the first tee dropped his bag and ran for

the parking lot," the *Patriot Ledger* mused), it gave a taste of true competition for women recently introduced to the game.

One woman not anywhere near new to the game was making her point all over that summer. Edith Baker stood on the ladies' tee at Scituate Country Club one windy day and announced, "I'll show you how to hit this thing in the wind!" She then stuck a five-iron line drive up against the pin and tapped it in for a birdie. The following week, standing on the 3rd tee at Oyster Harbors, Baker announced, "Watch me draw this shot into the pin!" and hit it into the hole.

In the Association Championship that summer of 1966, the tried and true met the up-and-coming with almost disastrous results. Played at Winchester Country Club, the event featured the usual nail-biting matches, right up to the finals, which paired Floss McClusky with 16-year old Pat O'Brien, a young lady who had been exposed to golf when her parents could not find a sitter and took her along while they played. Accustomed to playing at Pittsfield where she was the only junior girl member of the club, she was a formidable opponent for Flossie. The match was even on the 18th with both players lying four on the green. O'Brien dropped in a 12-foot putt, assumed she'd won, took off her hat, waved to the crowd, shook McClusky's hand and

WHAT WILL THEY WEAR?

"Maybe a good yardstick (for skirt length) would be a half an inch for every year over 16."

— *Kitte Desmond on fashion*

said "nice match." McClusky, looking confused, picked up her ball and walked off as the gallery watched, amazed.

O'Brien said later that she'd thought she was one up. McClusky said, "I never even thought of keeping score with all the officials around. Besides, I was having enough trouble wishing the ball into the hole." She said she thought her putt had been conceded. The Committee ruled both players were wrong and, citing the Equity Rule, sent the match into extra holes. It all ended on the 21st, where McClusky won. O'Brien said afterward that she'd just entered "for the experience." No one could deny it was an experience.

While O'Brien would have been the youngest player ever to win the Championship, she was not denied victory that year. She went on to win the Junior Championship. And, as the run-

ner up in the Association Championship, she was awarded the first-ever trophy dedicated to Margaret Curtis.

The 1960's closed out with more and more young golfers entering the WGAM field. One name on the junior roster for the first time in 1968 was Pat Bradley, and in 1969, Pat O'Brien did win the Association Championship. As the older women guided them, it became clear a new generation was coming on board. Still, there were to be struggles. Golf for women would never come easily. There would always be something to overcome — a need for courses, a battle for equity with the men. The women would prove they were up to the challenge. Consider this decade closer: Pippy Rooney O'Connor won the Cris Eaton in 1969 with her partner Cele (Mrs. John) Cahill. That victory came just eight weeks and three days after Pippy had given birth to her son Teddy. No man could brag of that feat!

❧❧

Entering the 1970's, the WGAM Board realized that the growth of the Association had to be controlled. With almost 2,000 members and fewer courses willing to take them on, something had to give. With deep regret, knowing the WGAM had been created to include all women who wanted to play golf, they voted a new tournament handicap cutoff of 22. The outcry of disappointment jarred

them, and they soon relaxed it to 26 and under for the Senior Championship and the Mother and Son Tournament.

In 1971, the WGAM lost its "personal computer" Eleanor LaBonte to complications from diabetes. While a true computer that calculated handicaps would soon take over her work, she would never be forgotten. The Fall Frolic was renamed The LaBonte in 1972. "She was so dedicated and self-effacing, we could seldom show our appreciation while she lived, " said Ann Grayson, WGAM President that year.

As the country struggled with many challenges to traditional standards, the WGAM was forced once again to reiterate its stance on golf fashion. Said one WGAM memo; "Scoop neck shirts, short shorts, tennis-length skirts and all tight-fitting apparel are considered inappropriate for the golf course." And while one member complained at a spring 1972 meeting that "this is a bit passé when you consider what lady pros are wearing," the WGAM stuck with its policies.

❧❧

This was to be the time of Pat Bradley and the WGAM was her proving ground. A New Hampshire girl, who started out skiing but discovered golf, Bradley came to Massachusetts because she was told she would find the best competition there. She held her own and then some. In 1972 she was named to the Griscom Cup Team, won the Association

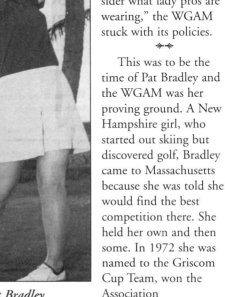

Pat Bradley

Caren McGhee (center)

Championship, the Stone Cup, the New England Women's Golf Association (NEWGA) Championship, and won the Endicott Cup handily. A focused young woman with her hopes set on a professional career, she did not stay long as an amateur. Still, she looks back to the WGAM to this day as providing the start that helped her become the LPGA Hall-of-Famer that she is. And the WGAM proudly followed her progress to her major world-class status.

Across the nation, issues of racial discrimination were challenging almost all traditional institutions. In 1972 Caren McGhee of Roxbury, a Metco student placed in Brookline High, became the first African American member of the WGAM. Asked about that status by the *Boston Globe*, the talented young woman said, "People don't say anything (when they see me). They just

walk into poles." McGhee, who won the WGAM Junior Championship in 1972, came to the sport blessed with both genetics and good coaching. Her grandfather, Henry Mason, was a club champion at Franklin Park and the great Pro Paul Harney took McGhee under his wing and coached her along. WGAM member Doreen Mowatt, also took an interest in Caren and encouraged her to participate in Junior and Association events.

In 1973 Pat Bradley continued her trek toward glory, winning the NEWGA Championship again. Clearly, she was going places.

As the energy crisis gripped the nation in 1973, going places was tough. Said WGAM President Ann Grayson at the annual meeting, "We may find the coming season challenging as we cope with the energy crisis and gas rationing." *Yankee Golfer* magazine agreed, writing, "The drive certainly will be the most important part of this year's game of golf . . . not from the tee but to the golf course."

Always proactive, the Board, led by

Nancy Black, set up more "regional" play for Spring Teams those years. Sure, they had to wait in lines for gas on assigned days and carpool more than ever, but the women didn't let a national gas crisis stop their momentum. If World War II hadn't, they vowed, this would not either.

Transportation was changing on the course as well. While the Association had long fought using golf carts for tournaments, in 1974 the Board ruled that motorized carts must be used if available. While they had always felt that caddies and walking were vital to the golf experience, they bowed to the trend for a number of reasons. Slow play was creeping in as a major issue and carts might speed up play. But more to the point, host clubs would make more money. Needing the cooperation of clubs, the Board made the concession, requiring the use of carts when clubs stipulated.

A happy note in 1975 was Dolly Sullivan's induction into the Northeastern University Athletic Hall of Fame. Sullivan, niece of golf great

Francis Ouimet and Dolly Sullivan

Ouimet Building Ground Breaking Ceremony - May 30, 1975
Left to right: Laura Parker, Mary Ellen Hurton, Gene Sarazen, Lorraine Sheeran,
and Gertie Cutler

Francis Ouimet, was never a nationally known competitor but locally she was held in great affection. With a strong game and a devotion to the sport, she had long worked with the WGAM to make women's golf more competitive and far reaching. Dolly loved nothing more than seeing a love of golf passed on to younger generations, just as it was to her. It is fitting that a special WGAM junior award is named for her. The Association was thrilled that their beloved Dolly had been so honored. That same year the WGAM office moved to the Francis Ouimet Museum Golf House in Weston, named after Dolly's uncle, who often played as her partner in WGAM mixed events. Dolly relished his affection even more than her own victories and honors.

When the U.S. Amateur Championship came to Brae Burn in the summer of 1975, the WGAM's strength and influence in the national golf scene was clear. With 150 starters, the field narrowed to the best of the best. Two of the final four were WGAM players, Noreen Friel, a 21-year old crack golfer from Woburn and 25-year old Jeanne-Marie Boylan of Charles River Country Club. Though both lost in the semifinals, it was one of the only times in memory two local women made it that far in the prestigious event. Fan loyalty was evident as well: the USGA reported the event drew the largest crowd to date at one of their events.

❧

By the late 1970's, the crushing need for tournament sites was on everyone's mind. Realizing they could no longer depend solely on the generosity of clubs, the Board voted a new policy requiring every member club to host a WGAM event once every five years. While they hoped this would make scheduling events simple, the struggle would continue into the future. With golf booming, it was frequently difficult to find a spot for the many events. Somehow, something always worked out.

The Association was focused on an important agenda: they wanted the Griscom Cup back. While strong teams had been sent to each annual competition, they had not held the coveted cup in 15 years. In 1977, led by team captain Gene (O'Neil) McAuliffe, the Massachusetts team faced off against rivals Philadelphia and New York at beautiful Oyster Harbors on Cape Cod. It was a cliffhanger, with the WGAM winning back the cup with 22 1/2 points over Philly's 21 and New York's 19 1/2. The WGAM was delirious with joy. The magnificent cup was filled with flowers and proudly displayed at the office the full year.

By 1978, close to 8,000 rounds of golf were hosted in a given year by the WGAM. Even with that huge number, the group remained tightly-knit, where friendships developed through competi-

tion. Kitte Desmond wrote, "The bonus of spring (matches) has been the number of lifelong golf friendships that have developed and built on the firm basis of courtesy, fair play and sportsmanship."

All of golf was benefiting from that facet of play. Women who met at WGAM events invited one another to member-guest events and to their home clubs. Others played rounds together just for fun. Tee times were even harder to get, golf shops were popping up everywhere and more and more women were turning on to golf. As one of a handful of associations in the nation at the time that accepted both public and private clubs to membership, the WGAM played a part in fueling a sports industry that would only develop faster as time went on. The boom continued, thanks in a giant part to the WGAM and the efforts of women like the Curtis sisters, Cris Eaton, and Eleanor LaBonte whom they had lost this decade but would never forget.

Ahead was even more evolution. As the group shifted to computers, modern machinery and the prospect of an even larger membership in the 80's and 90's, things would have to change. The question at that time was whether they could meet that challenge and still remain the warm intimate group of golf lovers they'd always been. Time and management would tell.

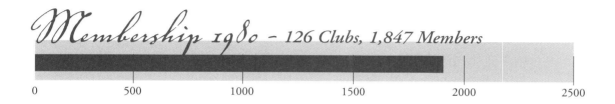

Membership 1980 – *126 Clubs, 1,847 Members*

Modern Times
THE 80'S AND 90'S

"Driving a golf ball into the next century may be dramatically different, but the game of golf should never lose its excellence of one-ness and the magic of winning."

—Kitte Desmond, WGAM Member and Boston Globe Columnist

Once the 1980's began, the women golfers of Massachusetts were inspired by world-class players such as Pat Bradley, and Sally Quinlan, the spirited Cape Cod girl and WGAM member who rocketed up the golf ladder from playing as a junior, to winning a golf scholarship, and to becoming a professional player.

Kitte Desmond

the year before. She played on the Dennis-Yarmouth High School boys' team and won a top position on that team. Quinlan's scrappy yet incredibly effective style put her at the top of the women's game.

"She appeared out of nowhere and what a phenomenon," said Anne Marie Tobin, who went on to win seven Association Championships herself. "She could hit the ball long, and I mean long. She just pounded it."

In stark contrast to the new "Young Urban Professionals" of the day who dressed the part before they had a game to match, Quinlan paid little attention to fashion trends or designer labels. Her talent and skill were what gave her style.

The WGAM understood that the clothes didn't always make the player. In fact, said Nancy Black, it was often the opposite. "Today's players have got the clothes and the clubs and they think that means they can play," said Black. Not so with Quinlan, whose most impressive accessory was her game. The WGAM members loved to watch her play.

The members also loved to test their own competitive skills. In 1980, the Association was forced to raise the Senior Championship age requirement

Sally Quinlan

Quinlan had closed out the 1970's by winning that decade's last Association Championship, having won the Junior Championship

to 55 because of over-subscription. Every tournament filled up quickly and with golf booming nationally, courses were even harder to find. By the time Gitty Scheft took over as president in 1982, finding courses willing to host all the Association events was even more an issue than it had ever been.

"I fear the almighty dollar overshadows the almighty lady golfer," member and future president Gertie Cutler quipped in 1982. She was referring to the unwillingness of more and more clubs to give up a day of player profits for a WGAM event. Another factor in this scarcity was that many first-timers were joining clubs. They didn't grow up with the game and had little or no respect for its traditions - like long-standing WGAM events. So the clubs weren't as willing to share their courses when their members weren't pressing them to do so. Indeed, golf's popularity was a double-edged sword and the burden of finding places for cup and tournament play for over 2,000 women continues to this day.

❧❦

The benefit of a membership eager for challenge was the quality of available competition. Tobin, who was and still is a keen competitor on the WGAM circuit, remembers the players who impressed her, like Noreen Friel.

Noreen Friel

"She was very learned, her swing was consistent and she was a classy person," said Tobin. She remembered playing Noreen for the first time in the early 1980's when Golf Digest ranked her one of the top 10 amateurs. "I was petrified. Here I was, this kid, playing against a Curtis Cup team member. I will tell you, she couldn't have been nicer."

Friel seemed to know how to win at any level. She could play whatever game

she needed on any given day. Players knew she was a woman who did what she had to and really knew how to win; a patient player who stayed strong from the first shot to the last. She went on to try the professional tour in 1983 but she chose to return to her amateur status in 1986.

And then there was Muffy Marlio, who rose to the top of the WGAM leader board in the early 1980's. Marlio's unique feature was her caddie – her caddie was always her husband. Her friends often teased her about that, but Marlio stuck with him with great results, hitting straight and working the course as one of the first true golf technicians. Marlio's style was to painstakingly pace off yardage for shots and to have a plan before swinging. She also had a way of creating a thrilling moment. Take the 1983 Association Championship. As defending champion, Marlio did not need to qualify and elected to be the first seed, playing the qualifying round for practice. It was her first time at Tedesco and she finished her round with a flourish, holing out from 75 yards for eagle on the 18th hole. She went on to win that championship.

Another player with a "double M" monogram was making a name for herself that decade as well. Marion (Maney) McInerney is quiet and sweet in person, but there is nothing shy about her game. By the late 1980's, it was clear she would be a force on the WGAM circuit. In 1992, she proved she would be that in an even wider circle when she became

Marion (Maney) McInerney, 1992 U.S. Mid-Amateur Champion, holds the cup donated by Mildred Prunaret in 1987.

the first amateur to win The Massachusetts Women's Open. That same year she won the Endicott Cup for the second time and then celebrated her wedding anniversary by winning the U.S. Women's Mid-Amateur Championship. *Golf Digest* named her as one of the Top 10 amateurs in the nation that year. No WGAM member had won a national event since Glenna Collett in 1928.

The national presence of the WGAM, which had begun with the Curtis sisters, remained strong with the fine play of these top Massachusetts competitors.

❧❦

On the regional level, the Griscom Cup had not lost its luster for the WGAM. Even with a team of excellent players, the WGAM knew they had great odds against them when they headed off to Rye, New York in the spring of 1990. The Bay State women had not won the cup in an away match since 1926. And while they'd won it at home in 1989, they'd not had back-to-back wins since 1911. To win it away and back-to-back seemed nearly impossible to the outsider. Not to the team – Anne Marie Tobin, Roberta Bolduc, Jean Enright, Natalie Galligan, Janice Golden, Marion McInerney, Kerry Lee O'Leary, and Carri Wood.

"We all just wanted to win so badly," said Tobin, who captained the 1990 team. "We all pitched in and it was a real team effort. It was what team golf really should be." The result was also what the Association craved. Massachusetts won, taking the trophy home for a glorious victory. The team reported that half the fun was working and traveling together. That thought echoes what Margaret Curtis once said about Griscom Cup events. "The fun of the Griscom in the horse and buggy days was the fact that the whole team

traveled to the matches on the same train. I can only hope the other occupants of the car forgave us our noise and good times," she said. That held true in 1990 as well.

The 1980's and 1990's saw a number of WGAM members turn professional. Leading the way was Quinlan. Having won the New England Women's Golf Association Championship in 1982, Quinlan felt sure of the hunch she'd had back in her early teens when she chose golf over her beloved tennis: she could play with the pros. She joined the professional tour in 1983, winning a tournament her rookie year and catching the attention of the nation. But the soft-spoken and unpretentious Quinlan did not find happiness. "For the first time, golf became a job," she said. Right off, she was harboring doubts about her decision. But she stuck with it. By 1989, however, it was clear she was not cut out for the tour. "I was driving home [from a tournament] and saw the sunset," she said, "and I pulled over and

burst into tears. It wasn't a good round; it wasn't a bad round. I just didn't want to do it anymore." And so, in 1989, the golden girl from the Cape called it quits. She now works at an AIDS spiritual resource center and says she feels completely fulfilled. In Pennsylvania, she is far from the greens of Massachusetts but what she learned as a WGAM player is with her today. Each year she organizes a golf tournament to help fund her AIDS program. It is there, and only there, that her golf life links with that of her new career.

"Boring."

-Shawn Chalmers describing her nine pars in a row at the 1991 Baker Cup

Besides Quinlan and Friel, others, too, made the leap to the professional tour, including Shawn Chalmers, Natalie Galligan, Marcia Melone, and Abigail Vernon, who tried the circuit and returned to their amateur status after several years. Jane Frost, Beth O'Kelly, Tara Joy, Justine Richards and Jean Enright tried the tour and instead became teaching pros. As of the year 2000, Melanie Curtin, Donna Glazer, Carri Wood, and Michelle Bell were all trying to make a name on the demanding and highly competitive circuit.

When it came down to it, what made the WGAM great — competition with camaraderie; high-level play with plenty of high fives — may have been what the women found lacking in the profes-

1990 Griscom Cup Team
Left to right: Carri Wood, Roberta Bolduc, Janice Golden, Natalie Galligan, Marion McInerney, Kerry Lee O'Leary, Jean Enright, Anne Marie Tobin

Anne Marie Tobin (left) receiving the Association Championship Bowl in 1988 for her first Association Championship win from Liz White, WGAM President 1988-89.

Left to right: Mary Wilkinson and Georgia Peirce with Anne Marie Tobin and Muffy Marlio - winners, at the 1986 Mildred Gardinor Prunaret Cup

sional ranks. On the greens of Massachusetts, the woman golfer could have it all.

Seeming to have it all through the 1980's and 1990's was one particular player, Anne Marie Tobin. She grew up playing at the Thomson Club, but it was in college that her golfing career really blossomed. In 1978 she won the Massachusetts Inter-collegiate Championship, the New England Women's Inter-collegiate Championship, and the Eastern Inter-collegiate Championship, a feat never before accomplished. Beginning in 1980, in two decades of WGAM tournaments, she won the Association Championship six times (five times consecutively), the Grace Keyes Cup five times, and the Baker Trophy once. During those decades, she was chosen for the Griscom Cup Team 14 times and captained the team twice. She won the 1983 Endicott Cup, and the 1990 NEWGA Championship. In 1990 she made it to the final 16 of the U.S. Women's Amateur and a month later to the quarterfinals in the U.S. Women's Mid-Amateur. The following summer she reached the quarterfinals of the U.S. Women's Amateur. Oh yes, and during those two decades she attended law school, passed the Bar and began a legal practice, served a term as President of the WGAM, and became a mother. In announcing the Player of the Year Award in 1994, Vice President Sally Fish warned the membership to "watch out for Anne Marie in her red Ford Bronco speeding into the parking lot, too late to practice, spikes untied, blowing dust off her 3-wood. We've only seen the beginning of Anne Marie Tobin."

While the young and powerful continued to make their names in golf in Massachusetts and nationally, one local name still grabbed headlines. Despite being two or three decades ahead of the new champions in age, Nancy Black was still claiming victories.

Roger Barry, golf editor of the *Patriot Ledger*, remembers watching Black with awe in senior, mixed and association championships in the 1980's and 1990's. "What impresses me about Nancy is the fact that she continues to play, and continues to play well," he

The 1999 First Cup on the first tee at Charles River Country Club.

The annual Spring Team competition remains at the heart of the WGAM tournament program. Changes in the last 20 years: 1980, camaraderie was enhanced when all teams in each cup were scheduled to play at the same course on the same day; 1981, the schedule was printed in the Blue Book for the first time; 1983, the scoring was changed from a three point Nassau to a point-per-hole; 1997, the debut of the Red Book.

said. "She is far and away the best golfer in terms of continuity. I can't think of anyone else who matches her." Indeed, since Nancy first won the WGAM Senior Championship in 1971, the engraver has scripted her name onto the bowl a total of 13 times, most recently in 1995.

Barry, who has watched Black win for nearly five decades, says, "I don't know of any other golfer who has played as long as Nancy as well as Nancy. She is a true champ!"

➷➹

While the exciting competition, the enthusiastic membership and full tournament rosters thrilled the WGAM,

"**Every golfer welcomes spring with open arms. But beware of those baring suntanned ones, especially if they are asking for strokes.**"

—*Kitte Desmond*

there were also many headaches for those administering the competitions. Through the 1980's, the WGAM was still calculating handicaps and arranging pairings by hand. Louise Mariani, an active volunteer at that time, remembers well the hard work that went into each event.

"Everything was done by committee and done by hand," the Halifax Country Club golfer and future WGAM president said. "The handicap committee would come in and check all the handicaps in a tournament to verify the index, and then each one had to be converted by hand to the course being played. Next the tournament committee would come in and do the pairings by hand. Talk about politics!"

The WGAM board felt simultaneously overworked and underutilized, and the strain of administering so many tournaments was beginning to show. They knew, Mariani said, something had to change. Technology would provide the solution.

It started, of course, with Mariani, who sat at a then modern Tandy Computer (now it would be called a dinosaur) and created a database of all WGAM members. It took her months, but it put the WGAM at the head of the pack when the USGA established a computerized handicap system and introduced its Tournament Pairings Program. Computers eventually calculated course handicaps, arranged pairings and greatly simplified scoring. "To say a revolution took place is probably minimizing the impact it had on golf," Mariani said. Today, most clubs have a computer on site and scores can be entered immediately after the

A course rating team in 1988.
Left to right: Sidney Arnold, Janet Peterson, and Louise Mariani

Janice Gannon Vance,
WGAM Executive Director

round. The GHIN program (and other similar programs) greatly facilitated accessibility and provided standardization of handicap records. Such modernization meant that the WGAM board was freed from its tedious tasks and could work toward a real goal: directing the WGAM into its future.

As office functions became more complex, the Board knew it was time to expand their staff. In September of 1991 they hired Janice Gannon Vance - the first full-time Executive Secretary to come from within the ranks. Vance, daughter of popular local golf professional, Larry Gannon, was the WGAM Junior Champion in 1959. She brought a strong game and knowledge of the sport to her position. In 1994, Vance was appointed the first Executive Director of the WGAM. She remains on staff in that position, working with every aspect of management of the Association. In the past few years,

Vance has overseen the creation of the WGAM web site and has implemented additional office automation. She coordinates the myriad details of tournament administration and her major challenge continues to be finding ways to fit all the avid women golfers into the tournament schedule. She is also a member of the USGA Regional Associations Committee, which enables her to better serve the WGAM.

Technology alone could not resolve the issues with course rating, however. As handicap calculations became more scientific, the accuracy of course ratings became more important. The only way to rate a course was to go there physically and examine every inch of it. The lengthy process took the teams well over four hours per course. Course and Slope ratings were then determined by tabulating lengthy columns of numbers with hand-held calculators. As a result, seldom were all the ratings up to date.

When the MGA was chosen by the USGA for a pilot program to standardize course ratings, Louise Mariani, who had been volunteering as a course rater, signed on to process the data. "The men's teams rated the course, had lunch, and then played golf," she explained. "The women's teams rated the course and then went home." The MGA had a much larger corps of volunteer raters.

When Mariani became President, Suzanne Nelson was elected to the Executive Committee as Chairman of Course Rating for the state. Despite her

54

best efforts to organize the process, it remained difficult for the WGAM rating teams to keep up with the demand for ratings. In 1996, it was finally decided to incorporate the WGAM rating program into that of the MGA. Today WGAM volunteer raters continue to assist MGA rating teams in a cooperative effort.

꙰

Outside of the WGAM, women were scrambling in a different way, demanding equal rights on the golf course. In 1998, the Executive Committee instituted a policy defining its stance against discrimination. With more women in the work force, the idea of men's tee times taking precedence over women's seemed outdated. While individual board members may have rankled personally at out-dated policies at their own clubs, the WGAM has tried to work with clubs to serve the overall interests of the membership.

The WGAM has worked in other ways, as well, to make the golf world more equitable for women. Under the guidance of Anne Marie Tobin and Jane Frost, the state's first girls-only golf scholarship was established in 1986. Frost, a local golf pro, had been holding a "golf marathon" to raise money for the WGAM junior program for years. Annually the group would use Frost's donation to purchase uniforms or some other items for junior teams. Then Tobin and Frost decided it was time to designate a more permanent use for the funds. With that, the WGAM Junior Scholarship Fund, Inc. was formed. While at first the revenue came from Frost, as years went on the WGAM became the major contributor.

A significant source of Fund revenues has come from the Dolly Sullivan Tournament. At the time of Dolly Sullivan's death in 1981, a group

calling themselves "The Friends of Dolly Sullivan" decided to begin a tournament in her honor. Club teams were invited to enter the first Dolly Sullivan Tournament, held at Halifax in 1982. Initially, proceeds from the event were contributed to the Francis Ouimet Scholarship Fund but after the formation of the WGAM Junior Scholarship Fund Inc., a portion of the proceeds went there as well. At the request of "The Friends," the WGAM took over the Dolly Sullivan tournament in 1994. Since then these proceeds have gone to the WGAM Junior Scholarship Fund, Inc. and the Francis Ouimet Scholarship Fund. In 1999, the Ouimet Fund, together with the WGAM and "The Friends of Dolly Sullivan," announced the establishment of the WGAM/Dolly Sullivan Restricted Fund, which grants scholarships to Ouimet scholars who

participated in the WGAM junior golf program. This restricted fund now also shares in the tournament proceeds.

The WGAM Junior Scholarship Fund, Inc. has also enjoyed the loyal and generous support of several member clubs who have made donations in lieu of favors at member-guest or invitational tournaments. Today, the WGAM Junior Scholarship Fund stands strong and has helped many WGAM juniors defray college expenses.

The influence of the Association could be seen in other venues as well. In October of 1982, the Massachusetts Golf Association voted to change their by-laws to include the President of the WGAM as an ex-officio member of their executive board. Gitty Scheft thus became the first female member of the MGA's board. While the two Associations had worked side by side for

Left to right: WGAM Presidents - Gitty Scheft (1982-83) and Janet Peterson (1980-81)

FIRST LADY HEAD PROFESSIONAL IN MASSACHUSETTS, Claudette A. LaBonte

In 1964, Miss LaBonte was the first woman in Massachusetts to become a teaching professional. LaBonte became the first woman Head Professional in Massachusetts in 1969. She was the Head Professional at Country Club of New Seabury from 1969 through 1971.

decades, Scheft's placement brought women into the boardroom of a group that controlled many aspects of golf in the state. Every WGAM President since has served as an ex-officio member of the MGA Board. Scheft also served for many years as a Director of the Francis Ouimet Scholarship Fund and in 1990 served a term as the first and only woman President of that Board.

Following her term as WGAM President, Anne Marie Tobin became the first woman to be elected in her own right as a regular member of the MGA governing Board.

In 1991, Mary Wilkinson (WGAM Junior Champion in 1976 – 77) became the new Head Professional at Salem Country Club. Her appointment was progress but as the *Boston Globe* noted, all was not well in the golf world for women. "But the juniors and the women still cannot tee it up on weekend mornings at Salem Country Club," the paper pointed out. Wilkinson was realistic, telling the *Globe*, "There are those who would automatically discredit me for knowing anything about golf because I am a woman. Sometimes you can change their minds. But there is always a faction who will never take you seriously."

⊷⊶

While the gender issues simmered, the competitive arena remained the true focus of WGAM activity. To keep the competition strong, the board knew they needed to bring more young women into the game. In 1992, while women were the fastest growing seg-

Above: Kelly Robb
Left: Kimberly Donovan

ment of the golf industry, the number of female golfers remained low. The WGAM had come to the realization that its membership was aging: only three percent of the members were in the 20-30 year range and another six percent were in the 30-40 year range. The Board knew they had to appeal to the young to keep women's golf growing, so they stepped up their efforts to improve the junior program.

The Junior Committee, led by Pippy Rooney O'Connor, began promoting junior events and increasing junior media coverage. O'Connor had a goal – to get girls involved at an even younger age. Her committee introduced the Mites Competition in 1988, a division for girls age 10 and under. While many came to events swinging clubs for the first time, the goal was not championship play, but rather building interest in the game. O'Connor knew just how to do that.

"Prizes, pictures and gifts," she said. "They go home feeling great and wanting to come back. That's the key." The junior events also allow non-club member girls to play, an important concept for bringing more girls into the game. It works. Consider Kimberly Donovan, a player with no club affiliation. At her first event, she could hardly swing a club, but leaving with a fistful of prizes, she looked up at her dad and said, "I really want to take up this game." She spent her winter on driving ranges and came back the next summer to win the Mites. In 2000, she was Junior-Junior Champion. "And she has many more championships left in her," said O'Connor.

Those girls will also have a good chance at college scholarships, O'Connor said. But what really makes O'Connor happy is seeing young girls hooked on the game that has made her own life so rich. "Before I go to heaven, that's what I wanted to do," she said.

The Junior Championships achieved their desired effect. With Junior, Junior-Junior, and Mite Championships, play improved and more girls turned out.

❧❦

The story of the final Association Championship of the century at Oak Hill Country Club includes all of the elements that defined women's golf in Massachusetts in the 20th century. The

32 qualifiers included five past champions - Tracy Welch, Karen Richardson, Mary Gale, Natalie Galligan, and Anne Marie Tobin. There was also a strong contingent of central Massachusetts local talent - including popular home

Left to right: Laura Torrisi, Joanne Catlin

course champion Joanne Catlin and Sterling Golf Club's Laura Torrisi. Twenty years old and a college junior, Torrisi had been the Junior Champion

in 1995 and 1996. She was a semi-finalist in the Association Championship in 1997, and was finalist in 1998, losing a heart breaker to Tracy Welch at Kernwood. She came to Oak Hill focused on one thing — victory.

The final match between Catlin and Torrisi was a thriller. Torrisi went one up with a birdie on the first hole but followed with three bogeys, a double bogey and two pars. Playing conservatively, Catlin strung together seven consecutive pars and made the turn three up. Walking to the tenth tee, Torrisi's caddie reminded her of the advantage of her length on the par fives and urged her to "play strong." She did just that — winning the par five 10th with a conceded two foot *eagle* putt. On the 15th hole, Torrisi drained a 60-foot birdie putt to pull even. She went one up for the first time since the first hole when Catlin conceded the 16th hole. On the 18th green, it looked like Torrisi would win her first WGAM Association Championship - until she missed a four-foot par putt and the match was all square.

The seven-hole playoff that followed was one of high drama. Each player had opportunities to win and both kept the gallery on an emotional roller coaster. No one watching will ever forget Catlin's near birdie on the third playoff hole. She had hooked her drive and punched out from the trees. Torrisi's second shot was safely on the green, 30 feet from the cup. Catlin's shot to the green clipped the top of the flagstick, hit at the back of the green and then spun back 15 feet to rest on the edge of the hole. Both players made par as the gallery caught its breath. The match was finally decided on the par five seventh playoff hole when Catlin's third shot failed to reach the green. Her pitch from the rough ran long; a chip back was short. Still away, she left her bogey putt short and conceded Torrisi's eight-foot par putt. She told the press, "I was getting tired and I just folded."

Ecstatic, the Champion Torrisi said, "Winning here in a play-off is the most thrilling experience I've ever had on a golf course. At any point in that play-off she [Catlin] could have won. She is an outstanding player. I have to say that was the greatest round of golf - match play, stroke play, anything."

What some watching did not know was that Torrisi and Catlin enjoyed a special friendship. Forty-one year old Catlin is a high-energy mother of three teenagers and a seasoned competitor. She had previously been the Championship finalist in 1981, was the qualifying medalist in 1994 and 1996, and had won the Endicott Cup in the fall of 1998. Torrisi comes from a large family where hard work and family ties are strongly valued. For the whole family, it is a source of great pride that Laura's skill as a golfer has made it possible for her to attend college with full scholarship assistance. Living near the Torrisi family, Catlin took an interest in Laura's progress and frequently gave her rides to tournaments, shared accommodations when travel was required, and offered friendly (almost motherly) advice. Catlin's 17-year-old daughter, Kylie, caddied

for Torrisi at the 1998 U.S. Women's Amateur Championship in Michigan when both Catlin and Torrisi qualified. Those in the gallery who were familiar with the special friendship between the two players could hardly root for one over the other.

> **"I never think of age when I am playing golf. I never feel older than my opponent. I love the game so much."**
>
> —*Fay DeRuvo, WGAM member*

Many in the gallery also knew that the Catlin family was struggling with a terrifying burden. Joanne's husband, Mike, had recently been diagnosed with leukemia. Though he still appeared healthy, he was fatigued and gravely ill and was undergoing treatment in preparation for a bone-marrow transplant scheduled for the fall. (Kylie would donate the marrow.) But that didn't keep him away from the course. On Tuesday, when Torrisi's caddie didn't show up for her first match, Mike hoist-

ed her bag! The next day he caddied for Joanne. On Thursday, after Joanne won the morning semi-final, Mike cancelled his 1:30 appointment with his doctor at New England Medical Center so that he could caddie in the final match. "I wouldn't have been able to stand it if I'd been driving back to Boston and she was playing," he told the Boston Globe. So he shouldered the bag again and stayed with Joanne through every shot of the grueling 25-hole match and play-off, refusing offers to hand over the bag to fresher legs. Exhausted after her defeat, Joanne told reporters, "That was pretty neat for [Michael] to do that. It was really special for him to do it this year. He was great. He was tired, but he wanted to do this so bad. I didn't expect him to be here. When he said he did it [canceled the appointment], it brought tears to my eyes. I really wanted to win it and couldn't do it. That's all right; we'll win something else more important. We'll win the other battle."

The final match of the 1999 WGAM Association Championship had it all - a seasoned, steady player challenged by an exciting, youthful talent, thrilling shot-making and heart-breaking lip-outs, and the unique camaraderie of golf opponents who are friends. To put it all in proper perspective, there was the drama of a courageous family — it is, after all, only a game.

⊰⊱

The Association approached the end of its first century preparing for what would lie ahead. In 1996 the WGAM moved to Highland Avenue in

---

GOOD SPORTSMANSHIP TIMES TEN

It was Louise Mariani's turn one day to total the Spring Teams scores for the day of play. At home doing the work, she realized she had inadvertently put herself at the wrong handicap, against the rules of the game. She immediately forfeited her match, causing her team to lose but to win as well. Mariani continues to be one of the most respected women in the WGAM. "I'll never forget that," said one member. "No one ever would have known, but Louise still did the right thing. That's what good golf is all about."

Needham, rejoining the MGA. Through a formal Agreement, re-negotiated annually, the two groups renewed their pledge to support one another. In 1998, led by President Suzanne Nelson, the Board voted to work toward building alliances with other women's golf groups that include higher handicap women. The intent would be to maintain the WGAM programs but also to provide the benefit of the Association's experience to other women golfers and to cultivate the interest of future members.

That same year the Board sought an objective evaluation of the Association and further understanding of the needs of the women golfers in the state. To accomplish this, MBA students at Babson College conducted a study of the membership. The high response rate showed the WGAM membership to be a loyal and satisfied base. The study found that while the WGAM catered primarily to those with handicaps 24 and lower, the majority of women golfers in Massachusetts were not eligible to play in WGAM events. The challenge is clear: to continue to be viable in its second century, the WGAM will need to find ways to bring young women into the game and keep them playing, despite the pressures of careers, family needs and all the trappings of modern life. The WGAM board agreed: that must be their goal in the new century.

The Annual Meeting on December 1, 1999 at Wellesley Country Club brought the first century of the WGAM to a close. In her remarks at that meeting, Nelson pointed out how dramatically the Association had changed since its

Suzanne Nelson, WGAM President 1998-99

founding and how future changes would keep it vital.

"Last year at the Annual Meeting in anticipation of the approaching Centennial, I talked a bit about some of the innovative things that the WGAM had done over the century to 'promote interest in women's golf'. And this year, I've tried to tie in bits of WGAM history as I introduced the various speakers and reports. My strategy in both instances was to show you how change has been a constant in the growth and development of the Association. Think about a couple of instances of how different the situation is today from 1900:

• In 1900, there were very few women playing golf anywhere. Every single member of the fledgling Women's Golf Association of Boston was a beginner. Promoting women's golf literally

meant putting a club in a woman's hands and pointing her in the right direction off the tee. In 1999, there are 6 million women playing golf in the United States, 23,000 women with GHIN handicaps in Massachusetts, and the WGAM program is for experienced competitors, not for beginners.

• In 1900, the WGAB sought to grow by recruiting members to swell its membership ranks. In 1999, while we welcome new members, we know that our traditional tournament program cannot be expanded much further and we worry that in order to grow we need to offer something more.

• In 1900, the WGAB was the only women's golf association in town. Now besides the WGAM, there is the very successful Executive Women's Golf Association, the Tour, SWInG, and many popular regional leagues. Through the Alliance of Women's Golf Organizations we have found a way to support the efforts of these groups and help make certain that women are finding their way into golf and to a group where they can play. Our role has clearly changed – we are no longer the only child, we are the older, wiser sibling.

What's ahead? I'm not sure but I do know it will mean more change. A century from now the WGAM probably will be as different from the way it is today as we are different from the Association founded in 1900.

What needs to endure are the things that got us through the first century of the Association – the unique and wonderful game of golf, and the firm conviction that women can play it well and deserve the opportunity to do so."

Signs of the Times

Some interesting firsts in golf and the WGAM in the 1980's and 1990's:

1980: The first year the word "liability" and "refer to our attorneys" appeared in meeting notes.

1981: The first year the Blue Book was labeled The Blue Book, though it had been called that since its inception in 1950.

1982: The first phone message recorder was installed in the WGAM office; the MGA held a workshop to learn about "the latest technology in golf handicapping - the in-house personal computer."

1983: The first ever Past Presidents' luncheon followed the annual meeting in December.

1984: The WGAM sweater debuted.

1985: The WGAM was incorporated.

1987: The USGA Slope System went into effect, the WGAM first used walkie-talkies and cast aluminum tee markers.

1988: The first May Jackson Award was announced.

1991: The WGAM began using a fax machine; however it belonged to the MGA.

1992: A laptop computer was purchased for on-site tournament work.

1994: The WGAM purchased its own fax machine.

1996: The WGAM hired its first P.J. Boatwright intern through a program funded by the USGA. Soft spikes premiered.

1997: The WGAM received additional computer equipment from the USGA.

1999: WGAM goes on line and launches website.

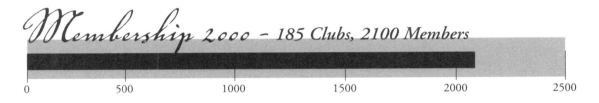

Membership 2000 – 185 Clubs, 2100 Members

| 0 | 500 | 1000 | 1500 | 2000 | 2500 |

Champions, Legends, & Ambassadors

"If all the women who have served as President of the WGAM were paid by the hour for their work, at the end of their term they could retire to the first tee and buy it."

—Kitte Desmond, 1973

What makes a champion? If the answer were as simple as the woman who wins the most tournaments at the highest level of play, the true champion of the WGAM would be obvious: **Pat Bradley.**

Pat Bradley, LPGA Hall of Fame member

To this day, Bradley is one of the best-known female professionals in golf history. She made her first mark in Massachusetts winning the WGAM Championship at Worcester Country Club in 1972. She now credits her early experiences on Massachusetts' traditional, classic courses with contributing to her success later on LPGA championship courses where shot making was essential.

On the LPGA tour, Bradley became

the first woman to win all four major championships, and she won three of those in one year, 1986. Her greatest battle, however, may have been with health. In the late 1980's her game started to slip and the press coverage was not sympathetic. When she finally realized that it was a medical problem and saw a doctor, she was diagnosed with hyperthyroidism. Medical treatment worked immediately and soon she was back on top. She handled that struggle with the grace of a champion.

Bradley set the bar for women professionals and it was another WGAM member who set the standard by which all in women's amateur golf are measured....
Glenna Collett Vare.

Glenna Collett began playing golf at the age of sixteen. Her debut in the 1918 Rhode Island Championship was less than auspicious. She finished with a score of 132...dead last. But three years later she won the WGAB Association Championship at Winchester, and that victory marked the start of an amateur career unmatched to this day.

In 1922, Glenna won the North and South Championship, the Eastern

Amateur and the U.S. Women's Amateur, which she would go on to win a record six times. Only Joanne Gunderson Carner, with a total of five titles, would come close to Glenna's record.

Glenna represented the United States in six Curtis Cup competitions, and served as captain an unmatched four times.

Perhaps her most enduring legacy was her unparalleled sportsmanship. In the introduction to Glenna's 1928 book, "Ladies in the Rough", Bobby Jones, the great male amateur, wrote, "Miss Collett typifies all that the word sportsmanship stands for." Many years later, in 1965, Glenna Collett Vare was honored by the USGA with its highest tribute, the coveted Bob Jones Award.

The LPGA honored her as well with the establishment of the

LADIES IN THE ROUGH

Glenna Collett
Pine Knoll December 17, 1928.

Pauline Mackay, winner of Association Championship in 1905 at Brae Burn, 1906 at Woodland.

Katherine Harley Jackson, winner of Association Championship in 1917 at Woodland.

Dorothy Campbell Hurd, winner of Association Championship in 1922 at Brae Burn, was one of the greatest international players of all time. In 1909, she became the first player to capture the United States, British, and Canadian Amateur Championships in the same year.

Marion Maney McInerney, 1987 WGAM Champion, won the 1992 U.S. Women's Mid-Amateur Championship in a thrilling 19-hole match against the legendary Carol Semple Thompson at Old Marsh Country Club, Florida. Marion's national championship was the first won by a WGAM member since Glenna Collett's 1928 U.S. Women's Amateur victory.

Another WGAM player to achieve national acclaim was **Joanne Goodwin**. In 1951 she emerged onto the WGAM golf scene to win the Junior

Championship for the first of four consecutive titles. Petite, demure, and shy in all other respects, she was anything but that on the golf course. Her game was one marked not by power, but by precision, accuracy, and intelligence. It was said by many of her peers that she could get up and down with a fairway wood more often than they could with a wedge.

When she outgrew the junior ranks, she wasted no time in establishing herself as the most dominant player in the area. Within a span of seven years, she won four WGAM Championships, seven Baker titles, the Keyes Cup, the Endicott Cup six times and the New

Vare Trophy, which is given each year to the player on the LPGA tour with the lowest stroke average.

While none have matched Glenna's record, six other WGAM Champions have captured USGA titles over the past century: **Pauline Mackay** won the U.S. Women's Amateur in 1905, **Harriot Curtis** won the title in 1906, **Margaret Curtis** in 1907, 1911, and 1912, **Katherine Harley Jackson** in 1908 and 1914 and **Dorothy Campbell Hurd** won it in 1909, 1910 and 1924.

Marion Maney McInerney with Carol Semple Thompson at U.S. Women's Mid-Amateur Championship in 1992.

*Curtis Cup players Joanne Goodwin and Noreen Friel Uihlein
at Evening of Champions July 25th, 2000 at Oakley.*

England Women's Golf Association Championship twice.

On the national level, she won the Doherty Championship in 1956, the Eastern Amateur in 1957, the International Four Ball in 1960, and nearly won the U.S. Women's Amateur in 1959, losing in the final to Barbara McIntire at Congressional Country Club, Washington, D.C.

She received the greatest honor a woman amateur can have when she was selected as a member of the 1960 U.S. Curtis Cup Team, captained by Mildred Prunaret.

Only one other WGAM member has ever been selected to play on a Curtis Cup team and that was **Noreen Friel Uihlein**. Noreen was a WGAM Junior Champion and won the Association Championship three times. On the national front, she won the Eastern in 1977 and was a semi-finalist in the 1975 U.S. Women's Amateur at Brae Burn. She was selected to play on the 1978 Curtis Cup team, a life-long goal.

⋨⋩

While the WGAM is proud of their relationships with these acclaimed players, they also hold in high regard "champions" of another sort, women who have played great golf while at the same time running tournaments, developing junior programs, serving on WGAM boards and in general, embracing the golfing life the membership loves so much. They are the Legends and Ambassadors of the Association's first century.

These are the women who have done what the six founding women pledged to do that March day in 1900. They worked hard to make sure the women of Massachusetts had "good golf and plenty of it."

Consider this roster:

Mildred Gardinor Prunaret was gentle, not dynamic in personal style but certainly dynamic in dedication and loyalty to the game. She never won an Association Championship (though she was the runner-up in 1933) and lacked the high level of play it took to be a Curtis Cup player. But her understanding of the game and how to bring out the best golf in others made her rise, with the rest of the cream, right to the top.

Mildred Prunaret served as Association President in 1950-1952, and then went on to serve as Chairman of the USGA Women's Committee in 1960. She donated the trophy for the U.S. Women's Mid-Amateur Championship, and it is known as the Mildred Prunaret Cup. She also served as non-playing Captain of the Curtis Cup Team in 1960, coaching her "seven dwarfs" as they were dubbed, including Joanne Goodwin and Judy Bell. Bell became the first woman President of the USGA in 1996. As if that weren't enough, Prunaret founded the Women's World Amateur Team Championships in 1964 and served as Captain in 1970.

While this work took Prunaret

Mildred Gardinor Prunaret

around the world, including a trip to Japan where she worked to develop women's interest in the game, her heart remained close to home, and home for her was the WGAM. She played in almost every tournament, and while her 8-10 handicap was impressive, it was her putting that wowed her friends.

"Her forte was definitely putting," said Nancy Black. "She had this rusty old putter that just worked for her and she'd pull it out and make the most amazing putts. Yet you'd never see her gloat after one, just smile happily. She was a prim and proper lady," Black said.

She made almost every meeting as well, pitching in with her experience and understanding to help the Association deal well with growing pains, financial issues and rules decisions. Her overall knowledge of the game was a powerful tool for WGAM members for decades.

Prunaret donated the WGAM Four-ball Trophy, a tournament now named in her honor. To this day, her name is known as one that made golf more competitive, more attainable and more fun for women in the Bay State and around the world. Other than Margaret Curtis, it's hard to find another woman who had a more positive impact on the sport. It might be said that her name alone helped WGAM women raise their level of play. At Wollaston Golf Club at the Four-ball Tournament in her name on July 30, 1990, two women scored a hole-in-one on the same day. Louise Mariani scored her ace on the 140-yard 12th hole and Denise Turcotte scored hers on the 120-yard sixth. To Prunaret, that would stand as the perfect tribute. She loved nothing more than influencing others to play their best.

Edith Noblit Baker was self-deprecating, smart, bossy and absolutely in

Edith Baker

love with the game. The junior girls under her wing referred to her as "Boss Baker," but with all the affection in the world. "You did what she said," remembered Pippy O'Connor, who was one of those juniors. "She bossed us, but in a very lovable way. You had to toe the line — manners, etiquette — but you were never allowed to be friendly on the green. I can't tell you how many times she told me, 'You were too friendly on the green!'"

Baker came to golf as a small child in Pennsylvania, where her father introduced her to the game. She remembered it as wryly as all else in life. "I started golf like everyone else. I picked up a club and played like a plumber."

A plumber, apparently, with an aptitude for the sport. By 1909, she was the Pennsylvania Regional Champion. By 1929 she had become a force on the New England circuit, having racked up

three consecutive WGAB Championships (a record that would stand for 65 years) and two Endicott Cup wins. Baker won her fifth and final Association Championship in 1932. Her best club then and to the end was her 'chipper.' "I think even now I could show these girls a little bit," she said in 1984.

Baker married and moved to the Boston area where she joined the WGAB right off and played as a member of Oakley Country Club. She dominated the Club Championship there for years, until she finally stepped aside, in true champion form, because she felt it unfair to the up-and-coming players. She stayed out of it for years, but in 1952, after two major back operations (one in which she asked the doctor to cut something to correct her overswing) she decided it was fair again and entered to play, hoping to challenge another player who had been dominating in her absence. Of course she won. When she donated the trophy for the club's women's championship, she specified that it was not a "memorial" because she was not "yet dead." Oakley's Championship is now known as the Baker Bowl.

For the WGAM, Baker did much more than golf. She served as Association President and worked tirelessly on programs. It was the junior program that was closest to her heart.

"She really loved us and called us 'her girls'," said O'Connor. " We all admired her so much. Some people were afraid of her, but you really had to know her. Her tournament, The Baker, was established for us, the working girls. We really appreciated that."

The Baker Trophy stands as one of the best-loved tournaments of the year. Slated for a "vacation-like spot" in the summer, it's meant to be a get away for working members. Until the day she died, Baker always made it to her tournament to oversee things each year. You can bet she made sure it was run right. Boss Baker would have it no other way.

Golf is, above all else, a game of manners, rules and etiquette. No player and WGAM member embodied that concept better than **May Jackson**. Jackson never won an Association Championship, but what she did win was the respect, loyalty and admiration of the entire Association.

"She was just an idol to a lot of us," said Pippy O'Connor, who played as a junior under Jackson's supervision and as an adult side by side with her. "She was a humble, beautiful person, and I mean beautiful not just in a physical way. She was a solid citizen, a person who stood up for what she believed in yet did it in the softest of ways."

Jackson was a player too. As a member of The Country Club and Wianno Golf Club, she won the club championship numerous times. In fact, she held the women's course record (72) at Wianno for three decades.

But it was her actions, not her swing that made her stand out. "She stood for what every golfer wanted, and still wants, to be," said O'Connor. "She was competitive, but in a quiet way. Her goal on the course was always to make you feel good. She was always complimenting your game, helping you to do better."

Thoughtful and unselfish, she put the wishes of others before her own. Many times when tournament enrollment was high, she'd pull herself out and put another golfer in her place, saying, "She deserves to get a chance to play." She served as a Griscom Cup captain yet was always humble about her play. She served as Association President 1948-1949 and on many WGAM com-

THE MAY JACKSON AWARD FOR EXCELLENCE BEYOND

The May Jackson Award, initiated at the annual meeting in 1988, honors outstanding women who have contributed to the growth and continuity of the WGAM. They have set the standard of excellence for all of us to follow. This is a very special award for very special people – like its namesake, May Jackson.

1988
May Jackson

1990
Nancy Black

1993
Kitte Desmond

1994
Mildred Prunaret

1996
Pippy Rooney O'Connor

1999
Gertie Cutler

mittees throughout the years, always lending her soft, confident voice to the issues at hand. Today, the May Jackson Award, given at the discretion of an appointed committee, is given when and only when a WGAM member emulates Jackson's ways. It is considered the most prestigious honor in the WGAM, and, as Jackson personified, it stands for all that is good about golf.

Frances Stebbins

Jeanne-Marie Boylan

Florence McClusky

Earlier chapters chronicle the influence of the **Curtis sisters** in WGAM history. Their role in the development of women's golf in Massachusetts, in the United States, and internationally cannot be overstated. As early visionaries, they helped to establish the tenor of outreach and philanthropy that is unique to the sport. Over the century many other WGAM members have worked beyond the state borders and have had appointments to the Committees of the USGA. **Fannie Osgood**, **Frances Stebbins**, and

Mildred Prunaret each served as the Chairman of a USGA Women's Committee. Like Prunaret, Stebbins captained a U.S. Curtis Cup Team – at Essex in 1938. As the WGAM enters its second century, eight Association members serve on various USGA committees.

In January 2000, **Jeanne-Marie Boylan** was elected to the USGA Executive Committee. In the 105-year history of the USGA, Boylan is the third woman elected to this elite group, following in the footsteps of Judy Bell (former USGA President) and Carol Semple Thompson. Boylan has served on the USGA Women's Committee since 1989 and has been the chair of the USGA Women's State Team Championship since 1995. Though several injuries have curtailed her play, Jeanne-Marie's competitive record is impressive. She won the WGAM Association Championship in 1975, 1976, and 1978, the Keyes in 1978, the Baker in 1975 and 1978, and the Endicott Cup in 1975 and 1977. She was a semi-finalist in the 1975 U.S. Women's Amateur at Brae Burn. Jeanne-Marie served on the WGAM Executive Committee for over ten years and is currently a trustee of the WGAM Junior Scholarship Fund, Inc. The WGAM is proud of her national prominence and

honored by her continued involvement in Association matters.

It was fitting that **Anne Marie Tobin** celebrated the Centennial by winning the 2000 Association Championship. She did it with flair, breaking the Oakley women's course record (74, set by Noreen Friel in 1974) with her medalist score of 72. This victory wasn't just a win; it was a win for the ages. With her victory, Tobin became the first woman to win the event seven times, and the second woman to win the event in three different decades, sharing this distinction with Florence McClusky. The Centennial Association Championship will be remembered not just for the celebration, but also for this player's remarkable achievement.

Anne Marie Tobin

Over its first century, the Association's Champions have set and achieved impressive goals, sometimes stretching over several decades. Consider these records:

"TRIPLE CROWN" WINNERS –
The Association Championship, the Keyes Cup and the Baker Trophy in a single season:

Joanne Goodwin
(1956)

Florence McClusky*
(1965)

Jeanne-Marie Boylan
(1978)

*Florence McClusky's winning record in WGAM major tournaments is unsurpassed with a total of 15 titles – five Association Championships, a record nine Keyes Cup wins, and one Baker Trophy. She won her last Championship at Winchester in 1966, twenty years after she first made it to the finals of that event. Hardly ready to retire, she went on to win the Senior Championship three times.

WINNERS OF THE ASSOCIATION CHAMPIONSHIP WHO ALSO SERVED AS ITS PRESIDENT:

	President	Champion
Grace Keyes	1902-1907	1900
Harriot Curtis	1915-1916	1920
Katherine Belcher	1921-1922, 1952-1953	1923
Fanny Osgood	1925-1929	1903-1904, 1910-11, 1913
Margaret Curtis	1938-1941	1901, 1907-08, 1914,
Deborah Verry	1942-1943	1937, 1940
Edith Baker	1946-1947	1925, 1927-29, 1932
Nancy Black	1968-1971	1946, 1947
Anne Marie Tobin*	1994-1995	1988, 1991-95, 2000

*Only one President has won the Championship while serving her elected term. Anne Marie Tobin managed this remarkable feat in both 1994 and 1995. Two Presidents captured the Senior Championship during their elected terms, Nancy Black in 1971 and Sally Fish in 1997.

WINNERS OF THE ASSOCIATION CHAMPIONSHIP MULTIPLE TIMES:

7 times	Anne Marie Tobin
5 times	Fanny Osgood, Edith N. Baker, Florence McClusky
4 times	Margaret Curtis, Dorothy Whittemore Beard, Joanne Goodwin, Dana Lombard
3 times	Rosamond Vahey, Noreen Friel (Uihlein), Jeanne-Marie Boylan
2 times	Molly Adams, Pauline Mackay, Vera Ramsey, Deborah Verry, Nancy Black, Patricia O'Brien, Debbie Simourian (Jamgochian), Muffy Marlio, Karen Plamondon Richardson.

WINNERS OF BOTH THE JUNIOR CHAMPIONSHIP AND THE ASSOCIATION CHAMPIONSHIP:

	Junior Championship	Association Championship
Dorothy Hunter Whittemore Beard	1930, 1931	1936, 1938, 1939, 1942
Gene O'Neil McAuliffe	1946	1960
Pippy Rooney O'Connor	1947	1955
Joanne Goodwin*	1951 – **1954**	**1954**, 1956, 1958, 1961
Dana Lombard	1956	1959, 1964, 1967, 1968
Patricia O'Brien	1966	1969, 1971
Noreen Friel Uihlein	1971	1973, 1980, 1981
Sally Quinlan	1978	1979
Loren Milhench le Gassick*	1983, **1985**	**1985**, 1986
Tracy Welch	1986	1998
Carri Wood	1988	1989
Laura Torrisi	1995, 1996	1999

Joanne Goodwin and Loren le Gassick share the distinction of having won both events in the same year.

WINNERS OF BOTH THE ASSOCIATION CHAMPIONSHIP AND THE SENIOR CHAMPIONSHIP:

	Association Championship	Senior Championship
Margaret Curtis	1901, 1907, 1908, 1914	1947, 1950
Ann Sampson	1963	1967, 1968, 1972, 1973
Florence McClusky	1948, 1953, 1962, 1965, 1966	1969, 1971, 1974
Nancy Black*	1946 - 1947	1971, 1975, 1977, 1978, 1981 – 84, 1986 – 88, 1993, 1995

*Nancy Black's Championship record is remarkable –
two Association Championships and 13 Senior Championships over a 49-year period.*

Association Champions at the Centennial Celebration, Oakley Country Club, July 2000.

Back Row: Left to right -Natalie Galligan, Mary Carr Gale, Debbie Simourian Jamgochian, Jeanne-Marie Boylan, Noreen Friel Uihlein Mohler, Pat O'Brien Dowd, Pat Bradley, Gene O'Neil McAuliffe, Anne Marie Tobin, Laura Torrisi, Karen Plamondon Richardson, Tracy Welch, Pippy Rooney O'Connor, Marion Maney McInerney, Loren Milhench le Gassick, Dana Lombard Aydelotte. Front Row: Left to right - Muffy Marlio, Ann Sampson, Barbara Thorner, Anne Nicolls, Laddie Homer, Nancy Black, Bea Bower, Joanne Goodwin.

These women – the Champions, Legends and Ambassadors of the WGAM, are the monuments of our past and the foundation of our future. Uncommon women, who over the span of a century, have been united by a common goal...

To play the game they love...
And to advance the game they play...

Women who, like the great Margaret Curtis,
can say without hesitation,

"Golf is my life and I love it. I'd play it with rocks if I had to."

So, WHAT IS IT THAT MAKES A CHAMPION?

Jane Frost - Keynote Speaker
Evening of Champions
Oakley Country Club
July 25, 2000

On July 25, 2000, following the qualifying round for the Centennial Association Championship, a gala Evening of Champions was held at Oakley Country Club, site of the 1900 and 2000 Championships. Jane Frost, nationally recognized teaching professional and special friend of the WGAM, gave an entertaining speech to the celebrants. She explained her view of "What Makes a Champion."

"What a tremendous honor to be here with all the champions - not only past champions but those of today and tomorrow. This is such a fabulous place to call home and I'm so glad that this is where I learned to play golf, where I fell in love with the history of the game and learned the many challenges that it offers.

From a teacher's perspective, it is not necessarily the fundamentals - although those are key. We need to have good FUNdamentals - with the emphasis on fun so that we do not become "duh-mental" about the game. Some of us have taken the game far too seriously. Please remember it is a game, it is recreation and we are there to recreate shot after shot, after glorious shot - the good ones, of course. Those who are champions do not talk about how miserably they are playing. They talk about the good shots. They talk about that wonderful putt that got them up and down and into the hole so that they made the cut into match play. This is part of the separation. Champions are very positive. So I took a moment and broke down the word champion and I took each letter and said, 'Well, what is it about champions that makes them different?'

C Champions have *confidence*. They do not go out there and think that they won't. If they did, they wouldn't! But they go out and think that they will and darned if they don't! They have *charisma*. They have that special spirit about them that takes them to the next level and allows them to hit shots that are just unbelievable to some of us. They have an amazing ability to *concentrate* and to focus on that one downhill 5-footer that they need to halve the hole. They are *charitable*. They give back to the game; they give back to humanity; they give back to their *community*. And certainly they are our *comrades*. On an evening like this, they are the ones say-

ing, 'Remember the time when…' and 'What a wonderful memory it is…'

H Champions are *honest*. They have honesty beyond reproach. They have a sense of *history*. They become enamored with the game and its traditions and they would like to be part of that history. They are pretty *happy* and they share that happiness and it becomes infectious amongst all of us. I found myself looking at that photo of a champion who is grinning and kissing the silver goblet and I said, 'Oh, how can you not be happy for that individual?' Above all, champions are *honorable*. I think of numerous occasions when we all had the opportunity to say, 'I didn't see that ball move.' Yet, we have taken a moment to be honorable in a world that seems filled with dishonesty. It is wonderful to be our own referee and say 'Oh no, that ball did move'.

A Champions *assess* the situation. They know when to take the opportunities and they know when to sit back and play it safe. They are *ambitious*. They certainly have goals and they want to get someplace. They may not readily admit it, but every champion out there has made it a goal to be the state champion. They have tackled that ambitious goal and hit ball after ball, and putt after putt. They are *altruistic*. They are willing to give back not only to the game but also to their peers and their comrades around them. They are truly *amazing*, *awesome*, and they *aspire* to go higher every time they go out to play. They challenge themselves to take it to another notch.

M Champions are *mature*, standing in front of a gallery and performing under pressure in front of all. They are *meticulous*. They take great care to prepare for the game and for the match at hand. Champions can be *mesmerizing* as we watch their ability to be one with the golf club and to swing in perfect harmony and send that ball exactly where they want it to go. They are *modest*. There is not a champion that doesn't downplay her achievements. Looking at the room full of the champions that stood before us tonight, we could see that they are all proud but also quite modest in their stance. And they are certainly *masterful* of all the shots, whether it is a chip or a putt or a blast from the sand.

P Champions are *playful*. Certainly, they get out onto the golf course and they play the game of golf. They are *polite*, knowing when it's their honor and when it's not. And it always seems that it is their honor. They are very *precise* about their game. Like a surgeon, they completely annihilate the golf course and take it apart. They are *passionate* about the game. They are *persistent*. They are very *positive*. And they *practice* with tremendous *pride*.

I Champions are *inspired* by a game of golf. They are extremely *insightful* as to their abilities and to what the game has brought to them. They are extremely *intuitive* as to what shot is appropriate for the situation. And when you take the word intuitive and take the first part of it, it is *in-to-it*. And a champion truly is - they are into the competition, into the golf course, they are into the spirit of the game. And they play that game with tremendous *integrity*.

O Oh, Champions are extremely *observant* and take the *opportunity* to go for it and to put the match away when the time is right. They *orchestrate* their game as they go around the golf course. They keep their minds *open* to the opportunities that are before them. They are the *ousters* that come before us! They are the people that send the rest of us to those consolation flights. And champions are truly *outcome oriented*. For they do have that goal and they know where they want to get by the end of their round.

N Champions are certainly far from *normal*. People often ask me, 'Is my grip normal?' I say, 'I don't know. What exactly is normal?' 'Normal' is only the setting on a dryer. 'Normal' is whatever you want it to be.

I would describe a champion as a *non-conformist*. For they take their level of competition, their level of play to something far beyond what we could ever imagine. They are *no-nonsense*. When they are competing they put on their game face and they are ready to go to work to really show us what a champion is all about. Champions are *notable* and they bring about tremendous *notoriety*. And they are *newsworthy*. They certainly have *nerves of steel*. They can stand there looking at that five-foot downhill putt and not break a sweat. Meanwhile I am looking for the closest towel to calm my nerves. They *nurture* themselves and their games around the course – again, knowing when to go for the end of the match and when to play it safe and bide their time.

C – H – A – M – P – I – O – N. It is a word formed of many letters; it is a goal built on many dreams; it is a golfer of many talents and special traits. Easy to spell, not hard to define, but oh, so hard to achieve.

I wish you all very well. Have a great week and play in the spirit of the game!"

PART TWO
THE CENTENNIAL CELEBRATION

The Centennial Celebration

W. G. A. M.

MEETINGS AND SEMINARS
- Anniversary Executive Committee Meeting
- Chairmen's Meeting/Seminars
- Annual Meeting and Past Presidents' Luncheon

CENTENNIAL EVENTS
- Luncheon
- Gala Evening of Champions
- Centennial Tournaments

TOURNAMENTS
- Spring Teams
- Association Championship
- State Team Competitions
- Tournaments

JUNIORS
- Junior Inter-City Team Matches
- Junior Tri-State Team Matches
- Junior, Junior-Junior & Mite Championships
- Mowatt Trophy

YEAR 2000 MEMBERS

WOMEN'S GOLF ASSOCIATION OF MASSACHUSETTS, INC.
1900 - 2000
100 Years of Serving Women's Amateur Golf

In March 1900, six women from four area clubs - Brae Burn, Concord, Oakley and The Country Club - gathered in Boston to promote the game of golf. They wanted to encourage more women to play the game, enjoy the sport and expand their own opportunities for competition. Consequently, the Women's Golf Association of Boston was formed to promote interest in women's golf. The WGAM has a long tradition of excellence in the sport. The roster of outstanding past WGAM members includes some of the most famous names in women's golf: Margaret and Harriot Curtis, Glenna Collett Vare, Mildred Gardinor Prunaret and Pat Bradley.

The Centennial Committee

Nancy Black	H. Louise Mariani	Gitty Scheft
Gertie Cutler	Suzanne Nelson	Lorraine Sheeran
Sally Fish	Jane Parker	Janet Sullivan
Sally Foehl	Janet Peterson	Anne Marie Tobin
Ann Grayson	Sandra Savian	Elizabeth White

MEETINGS AND SEMINARS
First Executive Committee Meeting
of the Women's Golf Association of Boston
March 5, 1900

In recognition of our official birthday, Carolyn Boday, Historian, read the minutes of the organizational meeting of six women, which was held at the home of Mrs. Kate Gannett Wells of 45 Commonwealth Avenue in Boston, for the purpose of forming a golf association among women. It was voted that the first Annual Meeting of the proposed Association be held on Monday, March 19, 1900, at half-past two o'clock. The Articles and By-laws were adopted at this meeting and the Association was declared as formed according to said Articles and By-laws.

During the Centennial Year the Bostonian Society approved a request by the WGAM that 45 Commonwealth Avenue be selected for the Boston Historic Marker Program. A commemorative plaque will be placed on this brownstone residence that was the site of the meeting at which the Women's Golf Association of Massachusetts was founded. To be so selected a location must have had "a significant and durable impact upon the history of the city". From that first meeting of six women on March 5, 1900 an impressive association of women golfers has grown and prospered, spreading its influence to thousands statewide and beyond-indeed, significant and durable!

45 Commonwealth Avenue

Anniversary Executive Committee Meeting
of the Women's Golf Association of Massachusetts
March 5, 2000

*Sally Foehl, WGAM President, 2000,
and Carolyn Boday, Historian, in 1900 finery*

*Sally and Carolyn displaying
Anniversary Cake*

*The Centennial Year's WGAM Executive Committee
L-R back row: Dori Frankel, Pamela Green, Kathrine Ranere, Nuala Pennington, Judith Norton, Maureen Berry,
Jill Finkelstein, Sue Tremallo, Jan Macallister, Marie Butera, Nicky Linehan, Alberta Endlar, Edwina Hughes.
L-R front row: Maureen Smith (P.J. Boatwright Intern), Elna Carlson, Sally Foehl, Susan Dean, Judy Keefe,
Janice Vance (Executive Director)*

CHAIRMEN'S MEETING

Excerpts from the minutes of the Chairmen's Meeting held at The Country Club on January 5, 2000: "A special thank you to Alberta Endlar for ordering our new WGAM Centennial Banner, which will be proudly flown at the tournament sites during this Centennial Year. Sally also recognized those members in attendance who belong to our four charter member clubs, Brae Burn Country Club, Concord Country Club, Oakley Country Club and The Country Club.... The tournament schedule for this year has most tournaments being held at the original sites. ...The handicap index eligibility limit has been raised from 28.4 to 30.4 for Spring Team participation. ...Guest Speaker was Genger A. Fahleson from the USGA discussing the 'Rules of Golf'..."

The Country Club, circa 1900, One of the Four Founding Clubs

Left to right: Sally Foehl, WGAM President; Genger Fahleson, USGA; Susan Dean, WGAM Vice President

SEMINARS

Jerry Green, member of the Massachusetts Golf Association's Executive Committee, with Nuala Pennington, WGAM Rules Chairperson (during a Rules Seminar at which Jerry was the instructor)

WGAM Rules Committee

Left to right: Christine Delany, Nicky Linehan, and Pat Berlo attending a Rules Seminar

Annual Meeting and Past Presidents' Luncheon

December 6, 2000

Brae Burn Country Club

Excerpts from the Minutes of the Annual Meeting:

"The Executive Committee of the Women's Golf Association of Massachusetts has, in the past 12 months, held twelve regularly scheduled business meetings and four special meetings. A total of twenty-eight motions were heard and twenty-seven approved. The Centennial Committee planned a year-long celebration for our 100th birthday - our 'Blue Book' turned 'white', the Centennial Calendar kept us informed as to Centennial events, The Massachusetts Golfer magazine covered our 100 years, Centennial bag tags were given to all WGAM members, the Centennial Book is in process..... Work continues on developing our Web Site... The membership roster of the Association at present includes 2,177 individual members and 182 member clubs. Twenty-four tournaments were held in 2000 involving fifty-two days of play. Spring Team matches numbered 171 teams, 855 players, competing in 29 cups with representation from 105 clubs."

Elna Carlson, Secretary

Jeanne-Marie Boylan, President of the WGAM Junior Scholarship Fund, Inc. announcing the Year 2000 awards

Barbara Locke accepting the Player of the Year Award on behalf of her daughter, Anne Marie Tobin, presented by Sue Tremallo.

Jan Bath, May Jackson Award Committee Chairman, paying tribute to May Jackson who passed away in August of this Centennial Year.

Honorary member, Kath Heffernan, oldest member, 'One month older than the WGAM' with Nancy Black, WGAM President, 1968-1971

ASSOCIATION PRESIDENTS

1900-1902	Mrs. Franz E. Zerrahn
1902-1907	Miss Grace Keyes
1907-1913	Miss Louisa A. Wells
1913-1914	Mrs. E. C. Wheeler, Jr
1915-1916	Miss Harriot I. Curtis
1917-1920	Miss Eleanor W. Allen
1921-1922	Mrs. Donald M. Belcher
1923-1924	Mrs. Raynor M. Gardiner
1925-1929	Miss Fanny C. Osgood
1930-1933	Miss Eleanor W. Allen
1934-1937	Miss Frances E. Stebbins
1938-1941	Miss Margaret Curtis
1942-1943	Miss Deborah Verry
1944-1945	Miss Frances E. Stebbins
1946-1947	Mrs. Edward H. Baker
1948-1949	Mrs. Henry B. Jackson
1950-1951	Mrs. Henri F. Prunaret
1952-1953	Mrs. Donald M. Belcher
1954	Miss Frances E. Stebbins
1954-1957	Mrs. Charles E. Eaton, Jr.
1958-1959	Mrs. Winthrop G. Dow
1960-1963	Mrs. Edward L. Peirson
1964-1965	Mrs. Vincent Farnsworth, Jr.
1966-1967	Mrs. Paul L. Hutchinson
1968-1971	Mrs. Paul G. Black
1972-1975	Mrs. Howard H. Grayson
1976-1977	Mrs. J. Paul Sheeran
1978-1979	Mrs. Samuel E. Cutler, Jr.
1980-1981	Mrs. E. Norman Peterson
1982-1983	Mrs. William Scheft
1984-1985	Mrs. John J. Sullivan
1986-1987	Mrs. David D. Parker
1988-1989	Mrs. Hathaway E. White
1990-1991	Mrs. Gregory Savian
1992-1993	Miss H. Louise Mariani
1994-1995	Mrs. James F. Tobin
1996-1997	Mrs. Robert L. Fish
1998-1999	Suzanne E. Nelson
2000	Sara Hastings Foehl

"PAST AND PRESENT W.G.A. PRESIDENTS line up for tea at 50th anniversary commemorating formation of Massachusetts golf group at The Country Club. Left to right—Eleanor W. Allen (pouring); Margaret Curtis, showing 1900 style; Mrs. Henry B. Jackson, Frances Stebbins, Mrs. Donald M. Belcher and Mrs. Henri Prunaret, present president."

Tribute to WGAM Association Presidents

Since 1900, thirty-five women have served as President of the Women's Golf Association of Massachusetts. Each President has dedicated years of volunteer service bringing wisdom, enthusiasm and expertise to the job of promoting amateur golf throughout Massachusetts.

Today, we have an association with golfers of all ages and ability enjoying the challenge of friendly competition and the camaraderie of those who love to play the game. How fortunate the WGAM is to have had a century of leaders who met the challenges of their day and paved the way for future WGAM Presidents.

CENTENNIAL EVENTS
CENTENNIAL LUNCHEON

WOMEN'S GOLF ASSOCIATION OF MASSACHUSETTS

CENTENNIAL LUNCHEON
Belmont Country Club
May 2, 2000

100th Anniversary of the first Spring Team Match

Master of Ceremonies:	*Jan Bath,* Women's Golf Association of Massachusetts
Champagne Toast:	*Sally Foehl,* President, Women's Golf Association of Massachusetts
Welcome:	*Jeffrey Ross,* President Belmont Country Club
	~ LUNCH ~
Introduction of Past Presidents:	*Jan Bath*
Anniversary Presentation:	*Jeanne-Marie Boylan* Executive Committee United States Golf Association
Archives Presentation:	*Rand Jerris,* Librarian/Historian United States Golf Association
Guest Speaker:	*Judy Bell,* Past President United States Golf Association

Centennial Luncheon Committee: Jan Bath, Nancy Black, Susan Dean, Alberta Endlar, Sally Foehl, Judy Keefe, Judy Norton, Jane Parker & Lorraine Sheeran

From Left: Jan Bath, Master of Ceremonies, with Janice Vance, WGAM Executive Director

Sally Foehl, WGAM President

CENTENNIAL LUNCHEON

Judy Bell, Guest Speaker
USGA Past President

Jeanne-Marie Boylan, USGA Executive Committee Member,
with Sally Foehl, WGAM President, in the background

WGAM Past Presidents with Judy
Bell and Jeanne-Marie Boylan

Back Row, Left to right:
Jane Parker, Janet Sullivan,
Suzanne Nelson, Anne Marie Tobin,
Janet Peterson, Ann Grayson, Elizabeth
White, Sally Fish

Front Row, Left to right:
Gertie Cutler, Jeanne-Marie Boylan,
Judy Bell, Sally Foehl, Nancy Black,
Lorraine Sheeran, H. Louise Mariani

CENTENNIAL LUNCHEON

Past Presidents L-R:
Liz White, Janet Sullivan, Janet Peterson

L-R: Caroyln O'Donnell,
Elna Carlson, Sidney Arnold

Sally Fish, Past President

L-R: Priscilla Neill, Helen Shean,
Ann McGuiggan

L-R: Helen Mullen,
Joanne Squillante

L-R: Edwina Hughes, Gail Jones

L-R: Nicky Linehan, Kitty Sturgis,
Susan Dean

L-R: Eleanor Beaty, Anne Dobson,
Ann McKissock

Past Presidents L-R: Gertie Cutler,
Nancy Black, Janet Sullivan

L-R: Karen Ammerman, Terry Berenson,
Molly Hoffman

Past Presidents L-R: Louise Mariani,
Suzanne Nelson

Association Champion Barbara Thorner
pointing out "Curtis Cupper"
Joanne Goodwin

CENTENNIAL LUNCHEON

*L-R: Rosie Morgan, Natalie Atwood,
Doris Hutcheson*

*L-R: Sally Agostino, Gloria Trovato,
Helen Vogel*

*L-R: Martha Speers, Jane Parker,
Gail Jones*

L-R: Marie Butera, Janet Peterson

*L-R: Barbara Thorner, Mary Rice, Ginny Pope,
Evelyn Baker*

*L-R: Nancy Black, Priscilla Bailey,
Alberta Endlar*

*L-R: Pippy O'Connor,
Jacqueline Cummings*

*L-R: Estelle Whitman, Karen Soloman,
Molly Hoffman, Tami Bane, Elaine Linsky*

*L-R: Marcia Yanofsky, Nancy Black,
Judy Keefe*

*L-R: Catherine Morat, Lorraine Sheeran,
Geraldine Rogers, Ursula Keleher*

Gala Evening of Champions

100 Years Ago from THE BOSTON HERALD
October 24, 1900

"Miss Grace B. Keyes of the Concord Golf Club is the champion of the Women's Golf Association of Boston. She won the honor Thursday in the final match by beating Miss Harriot S. Curtis of the Oakley Country Club, 5 up and 3 to play. The first championship of this new association, which thus comes to an end, has been a great success. It has added to the prestige of Oakley as a center of golfing activity, and has not only given the women of the Boston district a pleasant week of golf, but it has demonstrated the usefulness of the Association and the ability of the ladies to manage successfully an important golf tournament.. The matches have all been well handled, and the attention to rules, scoring, etc., …has been such as to afford an object lesson to tournament committees."

Jane Frost, guest speaker,
1994 LPGA Teacher of the Year

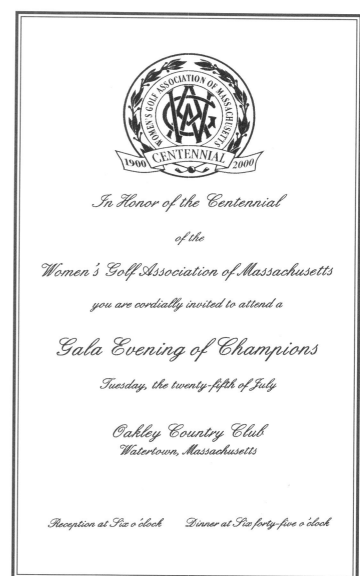

In Honor of the Centennial

of the

Women's Golf Association of Massachusetts

you are cordially invited to attend a

Gala Evening of Champions

Tuesday, the twenty-fifth of July

Oakley Country Club
Watertown, Massachusetts

Reception at Six o'clock   Dinner at Six forty-five o'clock

GALA EVENING OF CHAMPIONS

Oakley Country Club, Circa 1900
One of the Four Founding Clubs

Champions in attendance, Back row, left to right: Natalie Galligan (1990), Mary Carr Gale (1996), Debbie Simourian Jamgochian (1974, 1977), Jeanne-Marie Boylan (1975, 1976, 1978), Noreen Friel Uihlein Mohler (1973, 1980, 1981), Pat O'Brien Dowd (1969, 1971), Pat Bradley (1972), Gene O'Neil McAuliffe (1960), Anne Marie Tobin (1988, 1991-1995, 2000), Laura Torrisi (1998), Karen Plamondon Richardson (1984, 1997), Tracy Welch (1998), Pippy Rooney O'Connor (1955), Marion Maney McInerney (1987), Loren Milhench le Gassick (1985, 1986), Dana Lombard Aydelotte (1959, 1964, 1967, 1968). Front row, from left: Muffy Marlio (1982, 1983), Ann Sampson (1963), Barbara Thorner (1970), Anne Nicolls (1952), Laddie Homer (1951), Nancy Black (1946, 1947), Bea Bower (1957), Joanne Goodwin (1954, 1956, 1958, 1961).

GALA EVENING OF CHAMPIONS
WGAM ASSOCIATION CHAMPIONS

Anne Marie Tobin

Marion Maney McInerney

Pippy Rooney O'Connor

L-R: Gene McAuliffe, Nancy Black

Karen Plamondon Richardson

Laura Torrisi

Barbara Thorner

Anne Nicolls

Mary Gale

GALA EVENING OF CHAMPIONS
WGAM ASSOCIATION CHAMPIONS

Ann Sampson

Laddie Homer

L-R: Loren Milhench le Gassick, Tracy Welch

L-R: Muffy Marlio, Joanne Goodwin, Bea Bower

L-R: Dana Lombard Aydelotte, Nancy Black, Bea Bower

Natalie Galligan

L-R: Patricia O'Brien Dowd, Jeanne-Marie Boylan, Noreen Friel Uihlein Mohler, Pat Bradley, Debbie Simourian Jamgochian

GALA EVENING OF CHAMPIONS

Past President
Janet Sullivan

Medalist - Anne Marie Tobin
President - Sally Foehl

Jeanne-Marie Boylan

L-R: Susan Dean, Pat Bradley

L-R: Jan Bath, Nancy Black,
Olive Nolan, Claire Nolan

L-R: Melanie Curtin, Sally Foehl

Alberta Endlar

Past Presidents L-R:
Louise Mariani and Jane Parker

L-R: Chairman of the USGA Women's
Committee - Mary Capouch with USGA
Women's Mid-Amateur Championship
Committee member - Gertie Cutler

L-R: Fay DeRuvo,
Noreen Friel Uihlein Mohler

GALA EVENING OF CHAMPIONS

L-R: Past President - Louise Mariani,
Anne Sampson, Past President - Nancy Black

L-R: Priscilla Healey, Mary Keeffe,
Edwina Hughes

L-R: Carolyn Boday, Sally Foehl,
Janice Vance

L-R: Priscilla Healey,
Pat Bradley

L-R: Bea Bower, Past President - Ann
Grayson, Gene McAuliffe

James J. Tierney
Senior Sports Producer,
AT&T Broadband

L-R: Rose Langley, Carolyn O'Donnell,
Mary McAvoy

L-R: Eleanor Tietje, Jay Tracy - MGA Second
Vice President, Connie Tracy, Stephen Dooley -
MGA Treasurer, Thomas Landry - MGA
Executive Director

L-R: Sue Curtin, Melanie Curtin,
Karen Richardson

CENTENNIAL TOURNAMENTS
Hosted by Concord Country Club and Longmeadow Country Club

The guidelines put forth by the Centennial Tournament Committee were as follows: Players are strongly encouraged to dress in period clothing. The format is a two player scramble (50% of lower player's handicap). Please adhere to the following:

Tournament Committee: Gertie Cutler and Sally Fish

USGA 2000 - 2001 Rules in effect except for the following: Which were part of the Constitution, By-Laws and Rules Of the United States Golf Association
** 1900 **

1. If a competitor plays from outside the limits of the teeing ground, the penalty shall be disqualification.

2. When a competitor's ball is within 20 yards of the hole, the competitor <u>shall not</u> play until the flag has been removed, under penalty of one stroke.

3. A ball <u>may</u> be lifted out of a difficulty of any description, and teed if possible, behind it, under penalty of <u>two</u> strokes. If it be impossible to tee the ball behind the difficulty, it shall be teed as near as possible to the place where the ball lay, but not nearer the hole.

4. If a ball be driven out of bounds, a ball <u>shall be dropped</u> at the spot from which the stroke was played, under penalty of loss of distance.

CENTENNIAL TOURNAMENT AT CONCORD COUNTRY CLUB

Concord Country Club, circa 1900
One of the Four Founding Clubs

Competitors in their 1900 Finery

Carolyn Boday, WGAM Historian
" Making History"

Centennial Tournament at Concord Country Club

Doris Le Blanc and Mary Anne Skerry

Alberta Endlar

L-R: Ruth Ann Holzapfel and Susan Donahue

Fore!

CENTENNIAL TOURNAMENT AT CONCORD COUNTRY CLUB

Janice Vance and Sally Fish

Helen Mullen

Sally Foehl and Alberta Endlar

Terry Berenson and Tami Bane

Laurajean McDonald and
Jane Welch

97

CENTENNIAL TOURNAMENT AT CONCORD COUNTRY CLUB

Pamela Cote and Barbara Yozell

Pam Leger and Evelyn Baker

Joanne Field

Rita Duane and Carol Donovan

Gertie Cutler, Carolyn Boday,
and Sally Fish

Centennial Tournament at Longmeadow Country Club

DeeDee Bentley - daughter of Ruth Waldinger (wearing her mother's 1940's attire)

Polly Rice and Ruth Waldinger in the 1940's

CENTENNIAL TOURNAMENT AT LONGMEADOW COUNTRY CLUB

Joan Callahan and Marie Bradbury

Nuala Pennington, Kathy Nichol, and Sandra Kochan

Linda Belanger, Nicky Linehan, and Jane Balboni

Centennial Tournament at Longmeadow Country Club

Kathy Nichol, Sandra Kochan, and Cheryl Krueger

Roberta Bolduc and Sally Foehl

Cheryl Krueger and Connie Havican

Linda Belanger and Jane Balboni

Sally Foehl and Judy Keefe

Carolyn Boday

CENTENNIAL TOURNAMENT AT LONGMEADOW COUNTRY CLUB

L-R: Muffy Marlio and
Mimi Henderson

L-R: Judy DiDomenico and
Judy Keefe

L-R: Gertie Cutler and Judy
Krzynowek

L-R: Nicky Linehan and
Nuala Pennington

Sandra Kochan, Connie Havican, Cheryl Krueger,
and Kathy Nichol

TOURNAMENTS
SPRING TEAMS

TEAM COMPETITIONS

1900	
1	Cup
4	Teams
16	Players
3	Matches-May
3	Matches-October

2000	
29	Cups
171	Teams
860	Players
5	Matches
	April & May

Wednesday May 2. 1900.

The first of the team matches arranged by the Association were played, as follows: the day being fine.

The Country Club. vs. Brae-Burn at Brookline. C.C.

	Holes up		Holes up
Miss L. A. Wells	11	Mrs. Andrew B. Cobb.	0
Mrs. F. E. Zerrahn.	8	Mrs. Leonard Fowle.	0
Miss Alice Sargent.	7	Miss Margaret Cobb.	0
Mrs. Frank B. Bemis.	6	Mrs. H. L. Ayer.	0
	32		0

The Oakley Country Club vs. Concord Golf. Club. at Watertown

	Holes up		Holes up
Miss Pauline Mackay.	3	Miss Grace Keyes. defaulted.	
Miss Harriett Curtis.	0	Miss Gertrude Fiske	2
Miss Margaret Kennedy.	9	Miss Elizabeth Lawrence.	0
Miss Grace Stults.	7	Miss Ellen W. Joy.	0
	19.		2.

Total for matches.

The Country Club vs Brae-Burn.
Holes up for Country Club. 32.

The Oakley Country Club. vs. Concord. Golf Club.
Holes up for Oakley 19. — Concord 2.

2000 TOURNAMENT WINNERS

2000 Spring Team Match Results					
(TIE)	1st Cup	Salem #1	(TIE)	16th Cup	Wenham #2
		Springfield #1			Woburn
	2nd Cup	Concord #1		17th Cup	Kittansett
	3rd Cup	Wenham #1		18th Cup	Bass River
	4th Cup	Franklin #1		19th Cup	Springfield #2
	5th Cup	Cohasset #1		20th Cup	Walpole #1
	6th Cup	Green Hill		21st Cup	Westminster #2
	7th Cup	Oakley #1		22nd Cup	Nabnasset Lake #2
	8th Cup	Dennis Pines #1		23rd Cup	Foxborough #1
	9th Cup	Myopia		24th Cup	Poquoy Brook
	10th Cup	Needham #1		25th Cup	Oakley #2
	11th Cup	Hickory Ridge #2	(TIE)	26th Cup	White Cliffs #2
	12th Cup	Presidents #1			Weston #2
	13th Cup	Beverly		27th Cup	Presidents #3
	14th Cup	The Country Club #2		28th Cup	Hickory Ridge #3
	15th Cup	Worcester #2		29th Cup	Walpole #2

SPRING TEAMS

The Country Club's 1951 W. G. A. First Cup Champions line up at their home course after defeating Weston 10 – 5 to clinch the title.   Left to right: Mrs. Robert H. Morris, Mrs. George P. Buell, Mrs. Henry B. Jackson (Captain), Mrs. Willard Howard, and Mrs. Ralph A. Powers

Spring Team Match 1st Cup Winners - 1965, 1966, 1967, 1968
Winchester Country Club
Charlotte Davidson, Nancy Thomas, Kay Hood,
Shirley O'Connor, Edna Bentley

1999 Spring Team Matches

HATS OFF TO ALL SPRING TEAM PLAYERS WHO....
. left at the crack of dawn
. maneuvered through morning traffic
. traveled near and far
. provided keen team competition
. played challenging new courses in all kinds of weather
. enjoyed golf with friends, old and new
... ALL FOR THE "LOVE OF THE GAME"

1999 Spring Team Winners – FIRST CUP
Springfield Team #1
In alphabetical order: Debbie Chabot, Marianne Donohue, Jeanne Mersch,
Karen Podgorski and Andrea Russo

Spring Teams

1999 Spring Team Cup #2
Pleasant Valley Country Club – Team #1, Salem Country Club – Team #1, Vesper Country Club – Team #1,
Country Club of Halifax – Team #1, Kernwood Country Club – Team #1, Brae Burn Country Club – Team #1

1999 Spring Team Cup #19 – Sagamore Spring Golf Club.

SPRING TEAMS

1999 Spring Team Cup #24
Nabnasset Lake Country Club – Team #2, Concord Country Club – Team #3, Dedham Country and Polo Club – Team #3,
Wenham Country Club – Team #2, Tedesco Country Club – Team #2, Fresh Pond Golf Course

1999 Spring Team Cup #23
William J. Devine Golf Course – Team #2, Scituate Country Club, New Bedford Country Club – Team #3,
Needham Golf Club – Team #2, The Ridge Club – Team #2, Olde Barnstable Fairgrounds Golf Club

Spring Teams

1999 Spring Team Cup #9

Blue Hill Country Club – Team #1
Hyannisport Club – Team #1
Captains Golf Course – Team #2
Dennis Pines Golf Course – Team #1
Oyster Harbors Club
Cohasset Golf Club – Team #1

1999 Spring Team Cup #6

Green Hill Municipal Golf Course – Team #1
Pocasset Golf Club
Country Club of New Seabury
Cummaquid Golf Club – Team #1
Needham Golf Club – Team #1
Fall River Country Club – Team #1

ASSOCIATION CHAMPIONSHIP

Established in 1900 and held every year since except for the war years 1918, 1943 – 1945, the Association Championship is recognized as the women's amateur championship of Massachusetts. Since 1900 the Champion has received a gold medal presented by the Association. In 1927, when the Women's Golf Association of Boston became the Women's Golf Association of Massachusetts, a new championship bowl was presented at the Annual Meeting and the old cup was retired. In 1929, Louisa A. Wells presented the Osgood Memorial Cup,

in memory of Fanny Osgood, to be awarded to the low net qualifier. In 1966, using funds raised by the Curtis Bowl Tournament, the Association purchased the permanent runner-up trophy and named it the Margaret Curtis Memorial Trophy. In 1999, the WGAM Executive Committee voted to restructure the field to 32 qualifiers in each flight: the Championship Flight and the First Flight. They also voted to establish a "Presidents' Cup" to be awarded to the winner of the First Flight and donated the trophy.

Left to right front: WGAB Loving Cup 1900-1927 and the Association Championship Bowl   Left to right rear: Margaret Curtis Memorial Runner-up Tray and the Osgood Memorial Cup for Low Net

Grace B. Keyes, winner Inaugural Association Championship

YEAR 1900 CHAMPIONSHIP MEETING
THE WOMEN'S GOLF ASSOCIATION OF BOSTON

The *inaugural Association Championship* was hosted by Oakley Country Club.

Champion: Grace Keyes

Runner-up: Harriot Curtis

Miss Grace B. Keyes, Concord CC	Miss Keyes		
Miss Pauline Mackay, Oakley CC	1 Up		
		Miss Keyes	
Miss Elizabeth Porter, Oakley CC	Miss Porter	5 & 4	
Miss F. E. Zerrahn, The Country Club	5 & 4		Miss Keyes
			5 & 3
Miss Harriot Curtis, Oakley CC	Miss Curtis		
Miss N. C. Sargent, The Country Club	3 & 1		
		Miss Curtis	
Miss Gertrude Fiske, Concord CC	Miss Fiske	by default	
Miss Louisa A. Wells, The Country Club	1 Up		

ASSOCIATION CHAMPIONSHIP

Anne Marie Tobin, Year 2000 Association Champion
(for an unprecedented seventh time)
Established a course record with a score of 72 to win medalist honors.

Current Format: 18-hole stroke play qualifying round, followed by match play in two flights of 32

The *Year 2000 Association Championship* returned to Oakley Country Club.

Champion: Anne Marie Tobin of Bellevue Golf Club

Curtis Memorial Trophy: Tracy Welch of Winchester Country Club (Finalist)

Osgood Memorial Cup: Laura Orlen of The Orchards Golf Course (low net qualifier)

Presidents' Cup: cancelled due to inclement weather

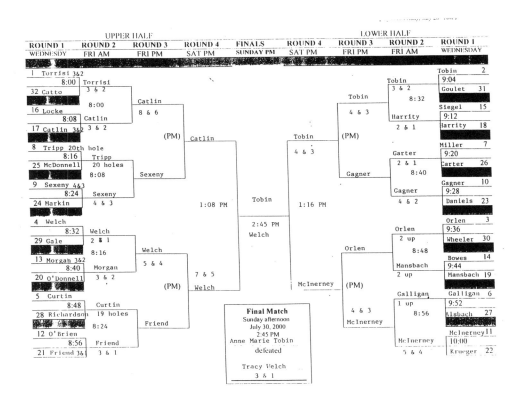

ASSOCIATION CHAMPIONSHIP

CHAMPIONS

Year	Winner	Site	Year	Winner	Site
1900	Grace Keyes	Oakley	1952	Anne Nicolls	The Country Club
1901	Margaret Curtis	The Country Club	1953	Florence McClusky	Winchester
1902	Mary B. Adams	Wollaston	1954	Joanne Goodwin	Essex
1903	Fanny C. Osgood	Oakley	1955	Pippy Rooney	Pine Brook
1904	Fanny C. Osgood	Wollaston	1956	Joanne Goodwin	Salem
1905	Pauline Mackay	Brae Burn	1957	Beatrice Bower	Belmont
1906	Pauline Mackay	Woodland	1958	Joanne Goodwin	Worcester
1907	Margaret Curtis	The Country Club	1959	Dana Lombard	Brae Burn
1908	Margaret Curtis	Brae Burn	1960	Gene McAuliffe	Concord
1909	Mary B. Adams	Oakley	1961	Joanne Goodwin	Charles River
1910	Fanny C. Osgood	Wollaston	1962	Florence McClusky	Kernwood
1911	Fanny C. Osgood	Oakley	1963	Ann Sampson	Haverhill
1912	Martha L. Roope	Wollaston	1964	Dana Lombard	Marshfield
1913	Fanny C. Osgood	Oakley	1965	Florence McClusky	The Country Club
1914	Margaret Curtis	Woodland	1966	Florence McClusky	Winchester
1915	Vera Ramsey	Brae Burn	1967	Dana Lombard	Brae Burn
1916	Vera Ramsey	The Country Club	1968	Dana Lombard	Nashawtuc
1917	Katherine H. Jackson	Woodland	1969	Patricia O'Brien	Dedham
1918	Cancelled – World War I		1970	Barbara Thorner	Tedesco
1919	Florence K. Daley	Brae Burn	1971	Patricia O'Brien	Charles River
1920	Harriot I. Curtis	Belmont Springs	1972	Pat Bradley	Worcester
1921	Glenna Collett	Winchester	1973	Noreen Friel	Pine Brook
1922	Dorothy C. Hurd	Brae Burn	1974	Debbie Simourian	Brae Burn
1923	Katherine E. Belcher	Worcester	1975	Jeanne-Marie Boylan	Weston
1924	Katherine Belcher Stone	The Country Club	1976	Jeanne-Marie Boylan	Winchester
1925	Edith N. Baker	Weston	1977	Debbie S. Jamgochian	Belmont
1926	Madeline Waxman	Kernwood	1978	Jeanne-Marie Boylan	Concord
1927	Edith N. Baker	Woodland	1979	Sally Quinlan	Salem
1928	Edith N. Baker	Weston	1980	Noreen Friel Uihlein	Duxbury
1929	Edith N. Baker	Charles River	1981	Noreen Friel Uihlein	Charles River
1930	Dorothy Richards	Salem	1982	Muffy Marlio	Dedham
1931	Rosamond Vahey	Brae Burn	1983	Muffy Marlio	Tedesco
1932	Edith N. Baker	Andover	1984	Karen Plamondon	Kittansett
1933	Mary Parkinson	Charles River	1985	Loren Milhench	Wollaston
1934	Rosamond Vahey	Winchester	1986	Loren Milhench	Walpole
1935	Rosamond Vahey	Brae Burn	1987	Marion Maney	Wellesley
1936	Dorothy H. Whittemore	Salem	1988	Anne Marie Tobin	Brae Burn
1937	Deborah Verry	The Country Club	1989	Carri Wood	Longmeadow
1938	Dorothy H. Beard	Belmont	1990	Natalie Galligan	The Country Club
1939	Dorothy H. Beard	Weston	1991	Anne Marie Tobin	Essex
1940	Deborah Verry	Worcester	1992	Anne Marie Tobin	Myopia
1941	Mary Grew	Winchester	1993	Anne Marie Tobin	Mount Pleasant
1942	Dorothy H. Beard	Brae Burn	1994	Anne Marie Tobin	Oak Hill
1943-45	Cancelled – World War II		1995	Anne Marie Tobin	The Orchards
1946	Nancy C. Black	Charles River	1996	Mary Gale	Belmont
1947	Nancy C. Black	Belmont	1997	Karen Richardson	Concord
1948	Florence McClusky	Weston	1998	Tracy Welch	Kernwood
1949	Ruth Woodward	Salem	1999	Laura Torrisi	Oak Hill
1950	Ann C. Boros	Brae Burn	2000	Anne Marie Tobin	Oakley
1951	Laddie Homer	Charles River			

Association Championship

Left to right: Marion Maney McInerney and Joanne Catlin, semi-finalists; Tracy Welch, finalist; Anne Marie Tobin, champion

Joanne Catlin (left) and Tracy Welch (right) during semi-final match

WGAM Committee Members, Left to right: Susan Dean, Gertie Cutler, Janice Vance, Judy Keefe, Sally Foehl

THE GRISCOM CUP

This rivalry started in 1898 as an inter-city match between The Women's Metropolitan Golf Association and The Women's Golf Association of Philadelphia. In 1900, Frances Griscom presented the Clement A. Griscom Cup on behalf of her father. Boston first joined New York and Philadelphia in the competition at Baltusrol in New Jersey in 1902. This tournament has been held every year since its 1898 origin, except for the war years: 1917-18, 1942-46, and one weather cancellation in 1984. From 1898 to 2000, New York has won 39 times, Philadelphia 32 and Massachusetts 24.

In the early years, the tournament was played over two days with 15 players per team. On the first day the two challenging teams played each other for the right to play the defending team on the second day. In 1910, the Associations voted to play 15 singles matches and six foursomes matches, with each city to play each other. From 1911 through 1916, the matches continued in this format with singles in the morning, foursomes in the afternoon. After WWI the matches resumed with just the 15 singles matches. In 1941, the number of players per team was cut to 11 players with all teams playing against one another in a single day. In 1952, the number of players per team was reduced to seven. In 1998, in celebration of the Griscom Cup centennial, the foursomes matches were reintroduced and the singles matches were increased to eight. Despite player enthusiasm for the enhanced camaraderie of partner play, only the eight singles matches were held in 1999. In 2000, the format returned to the eight singles matches and four foursomes matches.

Early on, interest developed in holding an individual championship in conjunction with the Griscom Cup competition. The Women's Eastern Golf Association was formed and the first Eastern Championship was held in 1906 immediately following the Griscom Cup. This event continued to be held at the same time and location as the Griscom Cup until 1951 when the two tournaments were scheduled separately.

Format: Negotiated every three years as part of the Inter-City Agreement, the format of the Griscom Cup has varied over the history of the competition. It always involves matches between players representing the three Associations. Players are chosen by their respective Associations.

The _**inaugural tournament**_ between New York and Philadelphia was hosted by Merion Golf Club, Haverford, PA
    Winner: Philadelphia

The _**Year 2000 Griscom Cup**_ was hosted by Brae Burn Country Club, West Newton, MA
    Winner: New York
    **Massachusetts team:** Roberta Bolduc, Joanne Catlin, Laura Day, Natalie Galligan, Marion McInerney, Karen Richardson, Anne Marie Tobin, Laura Torrisi, Abigail Vernon.

Brae Burn Country Club, circa 1900
One of the Four Founding Clubs

Sally Foehl (left) and Susan Dean (right)
holding the Griscom Cup cake

THE GRISCOM CUP

The Year 2000 Massachusetts Team
Left to right (back row): Karen Richardson, Joanne Catlin, Anne Marie Tobin, Laura Torrisi, Marion McInerney, Laura Day,
Abigail Vernon, Natalie Galligan, and Roberta Bolduc with team captains Robyn St. Clair and Marie Butera

Natalie Galligan reading the names on the Griscom Cup while Marion McInerney looks on in 1990

The Year 2000 Massachusetts Griscom Cup officials
Left to right: Sally Foehl, Robyn St. Clair, Marie Butera, Susan Dean, Gertie Cutler, and Janice Vance

THE ENDICOTT CUP

Established in 1926, the first Endicott Cup competition was a 36-hole stroke play competition between members of the Connecticut Women's Golf Association and the Women's Golf Association of Massachusetts. At that time, members of Rhode Island clubs belonged to the WGAM. The Endicott Cup was presented by Priscilla Maxwell Endicott with the understanding that the first person to win the tournament three times would retire the cup. When Edith Baker won the cup for the second time she asked that the trophy be perpetuated and the winner hold the cup for one year. In 1929, the Kittredge Cup, a match-play competition for the nine low gross players was added. In 1930, the Rhode Island Women's Golf Association joined the tournament. In 1932, the Kittredge Cup was retired and replaced by the Tri-State Trophy. In 1962, competition for the Eaton Trophy began. Originally this was a low-net contest played simultaneously by those competing for the Tri-State gross trophy. Since 1968, a separate team of players has been selected to represent each state in the Eaton Tri-State Handicap Matches.

Current Format: 36-hole individual stroke play tournament for the Endicott Cup. On the third day, each state fields two teams of seven players from the list of competitors from the first two days of play, to compete in the Tri-State and the Eaton team competitions.

The _inaugural tournament_ was hosted by the Hartford Country Club in Hartford, Connecticut.
  Winner: Edith Noblit Baker from Massachusetts

The _Year 2000 tournament_ was hosted by The Orchards Golf Course, South Hadley, Massachusetts.
  Winner: Anne Marie Tobin defeated Karen Richardson, defender, in a two-hole sudden-death playoff.

Tri-State Bowl: Massachusetts (Anne Marie Tobin, Karen Richardson, Dana Harrity, Kirsten Davis, Abigail Vernon, Christine Gagner, Marion McInerney, alternate: Martha Cain)

Eaton Tri-State Handicap Trophy: Massachusetts (Margie Riley, Gerry Baker, Fay DeRuvo, Cheryl Krueger, Penny Locke, Roberta Bolduc, Christine Coughlin, alternate: Inga Devenis)

WGAM MEMBERS WITH MULTIPLE ENDICOTT CUP WINS

Joanne Goodwin - 6 times
Dorothy Hunter Beard - 3 times
Edith Noblit Baker - 2 times
Jeanne-Marie Boylan - 2 times
Mary Carr Gale - 2 times
Marion Maney McInerney - 2 times
Anne Marie Tobin - 2 times

"The Endicott Cup is truly a fun tournament which not only provides a great format for excellent golf but good competition against one another in an effort to make the match play teams as well as keen competition with the other states. More importantly, it provides an excellent opportunity for camaraderie and to develop friendships with golfers from Connecticut and Rhode Island."

Marie Butera, Endicott Cup Captain - 2000

THE ENDICOTT CUP

Marie Butera, Captain, holding the Tri-State Bowl and Gerry Baker with the Eaton Tri-State Handicap Trophy, with teams

Left to right: Dana Harrity, Anne Marie Tobin and Karen Richardson

THE GRACE KEYES CUP

Established in 1950 when Grace Keyes presented The Keyes Cup to the Women's Golf Association of Massachusetts for an annual stroke play competition. From 1950 to 1957 the tournament was played as a 54-hole event. In 1958 the format changed to 36-holes. Miss Keyes, a member of Concord Country Club, was one of the six founding members of the Women's Golf Association of Boston in 1900 and was the winner of the first Association Championship. She served as President of the Association from 1902-1907.

Suzanne Nelson presenting the 1998 Keyes Cup Chair to Laura Torrisi

Current Format: 36-hole stroke play for Class A players

The *inaugural tournament* was hosted by Charles River Country Club.
>   *Winner:* Mary Gleason

The *Year 2000 tournament* returned to Charles River Country Club.
>   *Winner:* Anne Marie Tobin of Bellevue Golf Club

Anne Marie Tobin, Year 2000 winner

THE GRACE KEYES CUP TOURNAMENT WINNERS

Year	Winner	Site	Score	Year	Winner	Site	Score
1950	Mary Gleason	Charles River	246	1977	Jennifer Brown	Segregansett	159
1951	Laddie Homer	Dedham	237	1978	Jeanne-Marie Boylan	Wollaston	161
1952	Florence McClusky	Belmont	239	1979	Kathy DeBroux	New Seabury	152
1953	Pippy Rooney	Concord	240	1980	Noreen Friel Uihlein	Framingham	152
1954	Pippy Rooney	Brae Burn	244	1981	Mary Wilkinson	Hyannisport	153
1955	Florence McClusky	Winchester	247	1982	Anne Marie Tobin	Mount Pleasant	75
1956	Joanne Goodwin	Tedesco	233	1983	Anne Marie Tobin	Belmont	146
1957	Cancelled			1984	Marion Maney	Thorny Lea	153
1958	Gene McAuliffe	Brae Burn & Winchester	159	1985	Marion Maney	Weston	153
1959	Florence McClusky	Weston & Pine Brook	153	1986	Mary Carr Gale	Worcester	153
1960	Claudette Labonte	Charles River	159	1987	Beth O'Kelly	Pine Brook	153
1961	Florence McClusky	Brae Burn	160	1988	Anne Marie Tobin	Spring Valley	153
1962	Florence McClusky	Pine Brook	155	1989	Anne Marie Tobin &	Vesper	75
1963	Florence McClusky	Pleasant Valley	161		Marion Maney		
1964	Cancelled			1990	Marion Maney McInerney	Thorny Lea	150
1965	Florence McClusky	Wellesley	161	1991	Shawn Chalmers	Winchester	157
1966	Nancy Thomas	Weston	165	1992	Justine Richards	Wellesley	152
1967	Florence McClusky	Salem	163	1993	Jean Enright	Stow Acres	151
1968	Florence McClusky	Kernwood	159	1994	Kathy Rourke Natale	Tedesco	158
1969	Paula Brophy	Vesper	80	1995	Allisyn Jennings	Charles River	150
1970	Gene McAuliffe	Myopia	156	1996	Marion Maney McInerney	Brae Burn	149
1971	Nancy Black	Winchester	157	1997	Tara Joy	Longmeadow	141
1972	Noreen Friel	Marshfield	159	1998	Laura Torrisi	Salem	149
1973	Betty Donovan	Blue Hill	160	1999	Anne Marie Tobin	Pine Brook	146
1974	Noreen Friel	Cohasset	151	2000	Anne Marie Tobin	Charles River	148
1975	Debbie Simourian	Worcester	151				
1976	Jennifer Brown	Charles River	158				

THE CLASS B CHAMPIONSHIP

Established in 1951. Dorothea Howard of The Country Club donated the trophy for the Class B Championship. Initially the format of this Championship was match play, then it was changed several times between match play and stroke play. Since 1972, the format has remained as an 18-hole stroke play event.

Current Format: 18-hole stroke play

The _inaugural Class B Championship_ was hosted by Woodland Golf Club.
    Winner: Marjorie Collins

The _Year 2000 Class B Championship_ returned to Woodland Golf Club.
    Winner: Maureen Christmas of Maynard Country Club.

Anne Ravinski presenting trophy to Allon Pierce, 1980 winner

CLASS B CHAMPIONS

Year	Winner	Site	Year	Winner	Site
1951	Marjorie Collins	Woodland	1976	Mrs. Edward Stone	Meadow Brook
1952	Mrs. R. Kushmick	Salem	1977	Mrs. John Shaw	Lexington
1953	Mrs. C. D. Inman	Brae Burn	1978	Mrs. Francis Brown	Blue Hill
1954	Mrs. A. Steinert	Oakley	1979	Miss Gladys Robertson	Wenham
1955	Mrs. William Scheft	Winchester	1980	Mrs. George B. Pierce	Acoaxet
1956	Mrs. Albert Murphy	Brae Burn	1981	Mrs. Philip Doherty	Milton-Hoosic
1957	Mrs. A. Hurwitz	Weston	1982	Jane Davenport	Bear Hill
1958	Mrs. Wm. O. Nicolls	Salem	1983	Carol Quackenbush	Meadow Brook
1959	Elaine Rodman	Oakley	1984	Dorothy Koczera	Beverly
1960	Mrs. R. F. Woodman	Foxboro	1985	Carol Wright	Braintree
1961	Mrs. A. Steinert	Vesper	1986	Lois Keefe	Andover
1962	Mrs. F. Lanciana	Bellevue	1987	Mary Ann Soltys	Tatnuck
1963	Mrs. P. Sands &	Bear Hill	1988	Cassandra Costa	Reservation
	Mrs. R. Hansbury		1989	Bea Tosi	Holden Hills
1964	Mrs. J. A. Finnerty	Charles River	1990	Phyllis Molesworth	Franklin
1965	Edwina Hughes	Nashawtuc	1991	Mary Proal	Crystal Springs
1966	Mary McDonough	Spring Valley	1992	Mona Main	Ellinwood
1967	Mrs. Ed. Erban	Bellevue	1993	Sandra Jordan &	Acoaxet
1968	Shirley Watts	Glen Ellen		Virgina Williamson	
1969	Mrs. W. Hawkins	Bear Hill	1994	Lynda Bedard	South Shore
1970	Mrs. Thomas R. Olson	Needham	1995	Lynda Bedard	Halifax
1971	Laurajean Yurkstas	Easton	1996	Beverly Treannie	Tatnuck
1972	Carol Carcieri	Andover	1997	Jo Sizemore	Braintree
1973	Mrs. Alexander George	Ould Newbury	1998	Pat Garabedian	Meadow Brook
1974	Mrs. N. Lee Worth	Wellesley	1999	Sandra Robichaud	Stow Acres
1975	Miss Ellen Malloy	Oakley	2000	Maureen Christmas	Woodland

THE CLASS C CHAMPIONSHIP

Established in 1959. Initially, the format was match play, then it was changed several times between 36-hole stroke play and match play. In 1963, the event was played as a four-ball tournament. Since 1964 the format has remained as an 18-hole stroke play event. The trophy was donated by the Association.

Current Format: 18-hole stroke play

The *inaugural Class C Championship* was hosted by Haverhill Golf and Country Club.
  Winner: Mrs. James Neely

The *Year 2000 Class C Championship* was hosted by Woodland Golf Club.
  Winner: Diane Drury of Westminster Country Club

Diane Drury, Year 2000 winner, holding the trophy

CLASS C CHAMPIONS

Year	Winner	Site	Year	Winner	Site
1959	Mrs. James Neely	Haverhill	1979	Mrs. Stella Myshrall	North Andover
1960	Mrs. Jos. R. Ripa	Oakley	1980	Genie Young	Franklin
1961	Mrs. Wm Lucas	Framingham	1981	Betty Huntress	Tatnuck
1962	Miss Flora Skinner	Bear Hill	1982	Joanne Barnes	Bellevue
1963	Mrs. V. Waldon &	Segregansett	1983	Barbara Copeland	Walpole
	Mrs. J. Reeder		1984	Val Caverly	Beverly
1964	Mrs. Paul Lamothe	Charles River	1985	Polly Dodenhoff	Fall River
1965	Mrs. Paul Lamothe	Walpole	1986	Elaine Joseph	Oxford
1966	Mrs. John M. Slattery	Norfolk	1987	Nancy Fleming	Acoaxet
1967	Mrs. John Marshak	Meadow Brook	1988	Mrs. Donald Main	Highland
1968	Mrs. Leslie McKittrick	Hillview	1989	Marsha Hayward	Saddle Hill
1969	Mrs. Wm. Jefferson	Wellesley	1990	Pauline Meade	Fall River
1970	Mrs. Harold Simila	Holden	1991	Margaret Murphy	Allendale
1971	Mrs. Clive Fazioli	Ponkapoag	1992	Carol Armstrong	Cummaquid
1972	Mrs. Walter Korkuc	Segregansett	1993	Helen Vogel	Meadow Brook
1973	Mrs. Irvin Fuller	Spring Valley	1994	Nancy DaCosta	Dennis Highlands
1974	Mrs. Henry J. Riblet	Wellesley	1995	Bea Tosi	Halifax
1975	Mrs. Raymond Lawson	Oakley	1996	Helen Vogel	Tatnuck
1976	Mrs. Charles Eastman	Bear Hill	1997	Judith Gordon	Braintree
1977	Mrs. Robert Weiser	Juniper Hill	1998	Joanne Bouvier	Meadow Brook
1978	Mrs. Norman Morrison	Blue Hill	1999	Roberta McCann	Stow Acres
			2000	Diane Drury	Woodland

The Class D Championship

Established in 1966 when the Association revised the handicap classes. The trophy was donated by the Association in 1972.

Current Format: 18-hole stroke play

The *inaugural Class D Championship* was hosted by Sharon Country Club.
  Winner: Mrs. Robert Nelson

The *Year 2000 Class D Championship* was hosted by Sterling Country Club.
  Winner: Joan Morin of Walpole Country Club

Joan Morin, Year 2000 winner, holding the trophy

Class D Champions

Year	Winner	Site	Score	Year	Winner	Site	Score
1966	Mrs. Robert Nelson	Sharon	88	1983	Carol Zelck	Brockton	94
1967	Mrs. Charles Melshak	North Andover	89	1984	Betty Huntress	Andover	90
1968	Mrs. Robert Browne	Saddle Hill	89	1985	Agnes Dauphinais	Fall River	94
1969	Mrs. Frank Clark	Indian Meadows	97	1986	Ellen LeBlanc	Oxford	92
1970	Mrs. Willard Lewis	Putterham Meadows	91	1987	Barbara Alcott	Wampatuck	94
1971	Mrs. Willard Lewis	Meadow Brook	95	1988	Kathy Briggs	Needham	99
1972	Debbie Suvalle	Sharon	87	1989	Julie Rossi	Ould Newbury	94
1973	Mrs. Leslie George	Spring Valley	95	1990	Debbie Bass	Fall River	94
1974	Mrs. B. Crume Lamb	Tatnuck	95	1991	Priscilla Cornetta	Allendale	88
1975	Miss Debi Barnes	Thomson	82	1992	Ellen Tennihan	Cummaquid	95
1976	Mrs. Wm. Jefferson	Needham	96	1993	Terry LaFleur	Meadow Brook	90
1977	Mrs. Keith Jennings	Hillview	91	1994	Patricia Gillespie	Tatnuck	90
1978	Mrs. Donald Hammond	Norfolk	94	1995	Rita Duane	Halifax	89
1979	Mrs. James O'Regan	Winchendon	88	1996	Mary Ellen Ewen	Tatnuck	92
1980	Doris Reardon	Franklin	95	1997	Charlotte Forbes	Gardner	89
1981	Josephine Krovitz	Sharon	86	1998	Carmen Madore	Wampatuck	89
1982	Betty Huntress	Maynard	89	1999	Roberta McCann	Norfolk	93
				2000	Joan Morin	Sterling	84

THE CLASS E CHAMPIONSHIP

Established in 1966 when the Association created a 'new' Class E. This competition was not held between 1967 and 1994. Beth Nightingale donated the trophy in 1995 when the tournament was reinstated.

Current Format: 18-hole stroke play

The _**inaugural Class E Championship**_ was hosted by Ponkapoag Golf Club.
   Winner: Mrs. Jeanette Otery

The _**Year 2000 Class E Championship**_ was hosted by Sterling Country Club.
   Winner: Martha Akey of Crystal Springs Country Club

Martha Akey, Year 2000 winner, holding the trophy

CLASS E CHAMPIONS

Year	Winner	Site	Score
1966	Jeanette Otery	Ponkapoag	101
1967-1994	Not Held		
1995	Nancy Chagnot	Halifax	97
1996	Beatrice Westgate	Tatnuck	104
1997	Joyce Leary	Gardner	91
1998	Kathy Luccini	Wampatuck	95
1999	Marie Bedard	Norfolk	93
2000	Martha Akey	Sterling	96

THE CLASS E BETTER BALL

Established in 1999 after a Babson College study of women's golf in Massachusetts recommended that the Association provide more competitions for players with higher handicaps. Thus, the Class E Better Ball tournament was initiated.

Current Format: 18-hole four-ball stroke play, USGA Handicap index 28.5 to 30.4

The _**inaugural tournament**_ was hosted by Highland Country Club.
   Winners: Dorothy Ahlin and Glorian Brennan

The _**Year 2000 tournament**_ was cancelled.

THE SENIOR CHAMPIONSHIP

Established in 1946 when Misses Margaret and Harriot Curtis presented the Senior Bowl to the Women's Golf Association of Massachusetts, to be held for one year by the Senior Champion. The first event had 28 entries and only two caddies, since it was still wartime. Mrs. M. E. Philbrick presented the Senior Net Trophy in 1958. Initially the age for entry was 50 but this was changed to 55 in 1980 due to the large number of players in the 50-55 age bracket.

Current Format: 18-hole stroke play in class divisions
The *inaugural tournament* was hosted by Brae Burn Country Club.
   Winner: Mrs. Christopher Haigh

The *Year 2000 tournament* was hosted by The Kittansett Club.
   Winner: Roberta Bolduc of Longmeadow Country Club

Philbrick Trophy: Nancy Chagnot of Walpole Country Club

SENIOR CHAMPIONS

Year	Winner	Site	Score
1946	Mrs. Christopher Haigh	Brae Burn	
1947	Margaret Curtis	Brae Burn	
1948	Mrs. Patrick E. Hanaver	Brae Burn	
1949	Mrs. John D. Woodfin	Brae Burn	
1950	Margaret Curtis	Woodland	
1951	Mrs. William M. Austin	Brae Burn	
1952	Mrs. Roy Heffernan	Weston	
1953	Mrs. George Buell	Woodland	
1954	Mildred Prunaret	Weston	
1955	Mildred Prunaret	Oakley	
1956	Mrs. Chas. F. Bartholomew	The Country Club	
1957	Mrs. Chas. F. Bartholomew & Mrs. Charles F. Eaton	Brae Burn	
1958	Mrs. Roy Heffernan	Pine Brook	85
1959	Mrs. Chas. F. Bartholomew	Woodland	83
1960	Mrs. Chas. F. Bartholomew	Kernwood	81
1961	Mrs. Chas. F. Bartholomew	Weston	85
1962	Mrs. Willard Howard	Vesper	82
1963	Rose O'Neil	Charles River	80
1964	Mrs. Richard Hart	Brae Burn	82
1965	May Jackson	Belmont	82
1966	Mrs. Chapin Fay	Oak Hill	83
1967	Ann Sampson	Woodland	81
1968	Ann Sampson	Thomson	83
1969	Florence McClusky	Mt. Pleasant	85
1970	May Jackson	Halifax	80
1971	Nancy Black & Florence McClusky	Weston	81
1972	Mrs. Richard Hart & Ann Sampson	Salem	85
1973	Ann Sampson	Haverhill	78
1974	Florence McClusky	Pembroke	87
1975	Nancy Black	Halifax	79
1976	Eileen Kenefick	Hyannisport	80
1977	Nancy Black	Spring Valley	78
1978	Nancy Black	Eastward Ho!	82
1979	Eileen Kenefick	Wellesley	84
1980	Peggy Clark	Thomson	83
1981	Nancy Black	Wianno	78
1982	Nancy Black	Holden Hills	78
1983	Nancy Black	Pocasset	79
1984	Nancy Black	Marshfield	79
1985	Clara Keliinui	Indian Ridge	83
1986	Nancy Black	Kernwood	79
1987	Nancy Black	Cohasset	79
1988	Nancy Black	Mt. Pleasant	82
1989	Lois Rautiola	Beverly	81
1990	Fay DeRuvo	Blue Hill	76
1991	Eleanor Tietje	Oakley	85
1992	Betsy Perrott	Captains	79
1993	Nancy Black	Hatherly	81
1994	Mary Berman	Beverly	79
1995	Nancy Black	Nashawtuc	83
1996	Sally Fish	Worcester	81
1997	Betsy Perrott	Springfield	75
1998	Mary Berman	Lakeville	80
1999	Roberta Bolduc	Berkshire Hills	75
2000	Roberta Bolduc	Kittansett	84

Roberta Bolduc, Year 2000 Senior Champion

The high winds had the flags at 180 degrees. Rain was pouring and scores were soaring. The main challenge was to complete 18 holes of play.

THE ELEANOR W. ALLEN BOWL

Established in 1938. Eleanor W. Allen presented the Bowl to the Women's Golf Association of Massachusetts. Miss Allen served as President of the Association for eight years, 1917 – 1920 and 1930 – 1933. She also served on the USGA Women's Committee for many years. The Bowl was to be held by the winner of a singles match play "championship" event for Classes C and D. This policy prevailed from 1938 until 1953 when the format was changed to an 18-hole four-ball stroke play format.

Current Format: 18-hole four-ball stroke play

The _inaugural tournament_ was hosted by Oakley Country Club.
   Winner: Mrs. Ernest Hooton

The _Year 2000 tournament_ was hosted by Plymouth Country Club.
   Winners: Tie: Barbara Donelin and Marian Conroy of
                       Presidents Golf Course; Carla Wieners and
                       Muriel Hallet of Cummaquid Golf Club

Miss Eleanor W. Allen

THE EDITH NOBLIT BAKER TROPHY

Established in 1950. Edith Baker's wishes were that a 36-hole stroke play event be scheduled during the summer months so that students and businesswomen would be able to enter and caddies would be plentiful. She purposely did not designate this as a "cup" tournament as she intended to donate a trophy. For the 1950 event, Mrs. Baker donated a lovely bracelet. By tradition, the winner now keeps "the Baker Bracelet" for one year. In 2000, Marion Maney McInerney and William McInerney presented the WGAM with a permanent trophy for "The Baker".

Current Format: 36-hole stroke play

The *inaugural tournament* was hosted by Cohasset Golf Club.
 Winner: Nancy Black

The *Year 2000 tournament* returned to Cohasset Golf Club.
 Winner: Laura Torrisi of Sterling Country Club.

Edith Noblit Baker
WGAM President 1946-1947
Association Championship winner:
1925, 1927, 1928, 1929, 1932

Baker Bracelet (in the fore ground) with the Baker Trophy

Marion McInerney presenting the permanent Baker Trophy to Sally Foehl, WGAM President

Nancy Black, inaugural winner, presented with roses in recognition of her 50th year playing in "The Baker"

THE EDITH NOBLIT BAKER TROPHY WINNERS

Year	Winner	Site	Score	Year	Winner	Site	Score
1950	Nancy Black	Cohasset	160	1975	Jeanne-Marie Boylan	Hickory Ridge	154
1951	Nancy Black	Marshfield	161	1976	Debbie Simourian	Wianno	154
1952	Mary Gleason	Charles River	153	1977	Patricia O'Brien	Hatherly	151
1953	Pippy Rooney	Dedham	160	1978	Jeanne-Marie Boylan	Pocasset	151
1954	Gene McAuliffe	Kittansett	157	1979	Noreen Uihlein	Kittansett	154
1955	Joanne Goodwin	Myopia	156	1980	Muffy Marlio	Sankaty Head	160
1956	Joanne Goodwin	Wianno	152	1981	Noreen Uihlein	Worcester	148
1957	Joanne Goodwin	Cohasset	155	1982	Susan Brainard	Taconic	152
1958	Joanne Goodwin	Marshfield	153	1983	Kathy Vendetti	Oyster Harbors	154
1959	Joanne Goodwin	Hatherly	153	1984	Robin Auger	Eastward Ho!	155
1960	Gene McAuliffe	Woods Hole	153	1985	Muffy Marlio	New Seabury	152
1961	Gene McAuliffe	Woods Hole	75	1986	Marcia Melone	Sankaty Head	156
1962	Isabelle Boyden	Wianno	157	1987	Mary Gale	Hyannisport	154
1963	Nancy Black	Marshfield	159	1988	Marcia Melone	Hampden	147
1964	Claudette Labonte	Pittsfield	156	1989	Anne Marie Tobin	Kittansett	146
1965	Florence McClusky	Eastward Ho!	160	1990	Marion McInerney	Plymouth	147
1966	Patricia O'Brien	New Seabury	164	1991	Justine Richards	Orchards	144
1967	Nancy Black	Hyannisport	149	1992	Justine Richards	Sankaty Head	152
1968	Gene McAuliffe	Marshfield	81	1993	Jennifer Lasky	Hampden	151
1969	Patricia O'Brien	Oyster Harbors	162	1994	Laura Gilmore	Wianno	150
1970	Penny Fall	Pittsfield	151	1995	Marion McInerney	Kittansett	152
1971	Joanne Goodwin	Woods Hole	157	1996	Tracy Welch	Woods Hole	148
1972	Joanne Goodwin	Cummaquid	168	1997	Tara Joy	Marshfield	142
1973	Ruthann Donahue	Wahconah	154	1998	Laura Torrisi	Pittsfield	75
1974	Mary Carr	Allendale	159	1999	Melanie Curtin	Sankaty Head	147
				2000	Laura Torrisi	Cohasset	74

Laura Torrisi
Year 2000 winner

Joanne Goodwin,
seven-time winner

Gertie Cutler and Nancy Black

125

THE CURTIS BOWL

At the 1954 Annual Meeting of the WGAM, friends of Misses Harriot and Margaret Curtis announced the initiation of a tournament in their honor and presented "The Curtis Bowl." This trophy is a replica of the internationally known "Curtis Cup," which the sisters had presented to the USGA when they established the Curtis Cup biennial team matches between leading women amateur golfers from the United States and the British Isles. The "Bowl" is inscribed: "PRESENTED BY THEIR FRIENDS TO HARRIOT S. CURTIS - MARGARET CURTIS IN APPRECIATION OF THEIR INTEREST AND DEVOTION TO GOLF." The tournament is open to all members of the Association.

Current Format: 18-hole foursomes alternate drives

The _**inaugural tournament**_ was hosted by Essex County Club.
  Winners: Mildred Prunaret and Anne Nicolls

The _**Year 2000 tournament**_ was hosted by Myopia Hunt Club.
  Winners: Dana Harrity of Ferncroft Country Club and
Anne Marie Tobin of Bellevue Golf Club

Both days of the tournament were played in rain and drizzle. Many a team found hole 13 to be insurmountable. There definitely was "no rescue from the fescue" - the tournament committee strongly encouraged the use of 'provisionals'.

> _Margaret Curtis invited young Pippy Rooney to be her partner in the first Curtis Bowl tournament at Essex County Club. They were paired with Cris Eaton and her partner, Gene McAuliffe. When the foursome arrived at one par three, Margaret issued instructions to Pippy, "Don't hit it long; I don't want to have to go into those bushes back there. Don't hit it left; there's trouble over there. Don't hit it right; I can't walk down that hill. Don't leave it short; there's that big bunker there." Cris Eaton chuckled as Pippy stepped to the tee, "Well, Pippy, Good Luck!" she quipped._

Left to right: Dana Harrity, Bill Safrin (Myopia Golf Professional), Anne Marie Tobin being presented the "Curtis Bowl" by Kathrine Ranere, WGAM Committee member

CRIS EATON FOURSOMES

Established in 1966. Late in 1965, Priscilla Bailey, Nancy Black, Ann Dow, Dotty Howard, May Jackson, Gene McAuliffe, Pippy O'Connor, Harriet Rogers, Dolly Sullivan, and Betty Tarr asked the WGAM Executive Committee to establish an annual foursomes tournament as a memorial to their friend, Cris Eaton. Since its start, the format of the Eaton has remained Chapman format, with partners from different classes; C-D-E play on one day, A-B on another. Low gross and low net trophies for both divisions were purchased with donations from WGAM members.

<u>*Current Format:*</u> 18-hole foursomes Chapman format

The <u>***inaugural tournament***</u> was hosted by Marshfield Country Club.
 <u>*Winners:*</u> A-B Division: Mrs. Edward McAuliffe and Mrs. George Rockwell
 C-D-E Division: Mrs. Joseph Cunningham and Mrs. Joseph Murphy, Jr.

The <u>***Year 2000 tournament***</u> was hosted by the Duxbury Yacht Club (Cris Eaton had been a longtime member).
 <u>*Winners:*</u> A-B Division: Diane Harber & Gayle Maroon Johnson of Thorny Lea Golf Club
 C-D-E Division: Tracy Cote & Donna McEvoy of Duxbury Yacht Club

Cris Eaton
WGAM President 1954-1957

Joe Eaton, Cris Eaton's son, presenting trophy to Tracy Cote and Donna McEvoy from Duxbury Yacht Club, Class C-D-E winners.

Joe Eaton and Sidney Arnold holding the plaque presented to DuxburyYacht Club by the WGAM in appreciation for hosting the Year 2000 tournament

Cris Eaton's grandson, Brad White, pictured here with WGAM Tournament Committee members, Judy Norton (left) and Alberta Endlar (right)

Joe Eaton, having a good time assisting with awarding prizes to Pat Berlo and Joan Embree

MILDRED GARDINOR PRUNARET CUP

Established in 1953 as the Class A four-ball match-play tournament, the event was renamed in 1981 upon the presentation of the trophy by the friends of Mildred Gardinor Prunaret. Mrs. Prunaret was president of the Association from 1950 –1951. Her many contributions to the golf world included: Chairman of the USGA Women's Committee, Captain of the U.S. Curtis Cup Team in 1960, an organizer of the Women's World Team Championship in 1964 and Captain of the U.S. Team for the Women's World Team Competition in 1970.

Current Format: Four-ball matches played at scratch. Flights of eight teams arranged according to handicap index totals.

The *inaugural tournament* was hosted by Blue Hill Country Club.
> *Winners:* Gene McAuliffe and Pippy Rooney

The *Year 2000 tournament* returned to Blue Hill Country Club.
> *Winners:* First Flight: Anne Marie Tobin of Bellevue Golf Club and Dana Harrity of Ferncroft Country Club

Mrs. Mildred Gardinor Prunaret

Mrs. M'Auliffe, Miss Rooney WGA Winners

CANTON, June 11 — Pippy Rooney and Mrs. Edward J. McAuliffe of Charles River won the WGA's first match four-ball tournament at the Blue Hills Country Club with a 21st hole decision over Mrs. Willard Howard of The Country Club anud Mrs. Winthrop G. Dow of Dedham today in one of the most thrilling matches ever sponsored by the association.

All four players had starry moments before Miss Rooney's par four on the third extra hole, a 403-yarder, finally decided the outcome. Twice, Mrs. Howard and Mrs. Dow were able to build a two-up lead, but the hard hitters from Charles River were able to come back and level the match at a later juncture. The medal scores for the regulation 18 holes for each side, three over women's par for the rugged Canton layout.

The cards:

Par out	545 354 355—39	
Rooney-McAuliffe out	354 373 365—43	
Howard-Dow out	456 454 355—41	
Par in	355 354 345—39—78	
Rooney-McAuliffe in	545 454 245—38—81	
Howard-Dow in	646 344 355—40—81	
Extra holes		
Rooney-McAuliffe	434	
Howard-Dow	455	

Mrs. Mary Gleason of The Country Club and Mrs. C. F. Bartholomew of Dedham defeated Mrs. Henry B. Jackson of The Country Club and Mrs. William Austin of Dedham, 7 and 5, in the consolation match.

THE HANNAH D. TOWNSHEND CUP

Established in 1930 when Hannah D. Townshend (Mrs. Henry H.) presented The Townshend Cup to the Women's Golf Association of Massachusetts in memory of her twin sister, Miss Fanny Osgood. Miss Osgood was the first five-time winner of the Association Championship. She served as the first chairman of the USGA Women's Committee from 1917 to 1919, and she served as President of the Association from 1925 to 1929. The Cup was to be held for one year by the player with the best 36-hole score in a competition for Classes A and B. This policy prevailed until 1934 when the format was changed to 18-hole foursomes with partners from the same club. The format changed back and forth between the foursomes format and four-ball stroke play with club pairs. In 1944, the format settled into a four-ball form of play, with partners from any club.

Current Format: 18-hole four-ball stroke play, Classes A and B

The _inaugural tournament_ was hosted by Essex County Club.
   Winner: Dorothy Hunter

The _Year 2000 tournament_ was hosted by Weston Golf Club.
   Winners: Anne Marie Tobin of Bellevue Golf Club and Dana
            Harrity of Ferncroft Country Club

Dorothy Hunter,
winner, inaugural tournament

Fanny C. Osgood

The Townshend Cup

Eleanor I. LaBonte Golf Tournament

Established in 1950 as a tournament to commemorate the 50th anniversary of the WGAM and continued as a "no fee" invitational four-ball stroke play event with Classes A-B on one day and C-D on another. In 1965, the name was changed to "The Fall Frolic". In 1968, the tournament was opened to all handicap classes with no restriction on partner's handicap class. In 1972, the WGAM donated a new trophy and the tournament was renamed in honor of Miss LaBonte who served as Executive Secretary of the Women's Golf Association of Massachusetts for over 25 years and handicap chairman for 33 years.

Current Format: 18-hole four-ball stroke play

The _inaugural tournament_ was hosted by Oakley Country Club.
    Winners: A-B: Nancy Black and Florence McClusky
                 C-D: Mrs. Ernest Hooton and Muriel Chadsey

The _Year 2000 tournament_ was hosted by Gardner Municipal Golf Course.
    Winners: Joanne Catlin and Susan Lemay of Oak Hill Country Club

Despite three days of rain, the tournament was well attended.

Susan Lemay and Joanne Catlin

THE BOSTON DAILY GLOBE— FRIDAY, DECEMBER 2, 1949

(Globe Staff Photo By Charles McCormick)
WOMEN GOLF HEADS—Newly elected officers of the Massachusetts W. G. A. Left to right, Miss Eleanor LaBonte, Newton Centre, executive secretary; Mrs. Edward Pearson, Salem, vice president; Mrs. Henri Prunaret, Natick, president; Mrs. Edward H. Bailey, Wellesley, secretary; Mrs. Ernest A. Hooton, Cambridge, treasurer.

THE SHEERAN TROPHY

The Executive Committee established the Husband and Wife Tournament in 1959. Dr. and Mrs. J. Paul Sheeran from Winchester Country Club donated the trophy in 1972 and the tournament was renamed the Sheeran Trophy in 1983. Mrs. (Lorraine) Sheeran was Association President from 1976 – 1977 and has remained an active member. She also served on the USGA Senior Women's Championship Committee from 1985 – 1993.

Current Format: 18-hole mixed foursomes, selected drives for husband and wife

The *inaugural tournament* was hosted by Tedesco Country Club.
   Winners: Bea and Albert Bower

The *Year 2000 tournament* was hosted by Winchester Country Club.
   Winners: Linda & Scott Hartz of Duxbury Yacht Club

Bowers Captures Tedesco H-W Golf

MARBLEHEAD—Mr. and Mrs. Albert Bower of Essex posted a 76 to win gross honors in the first W.G.A. husband and wife tournament at Tedesco Country Club Friday. One hundred teams participated in the 18-hole medal play event of selected drives and alternate shots, as well as the Callaway handicap system.

Mr. and Mrs. Richard Hart of Wenham took second gross honors with 79. Mr. and Mrs. Douglas Doherty of Cohasset and Mr. and Mrs. Lester Sobin of Belmont were tied fo rthird gross at 82.

Net honors were divided among Mr. and Mrs. Harry A. Hood of Winchester (81-71), Mr. and Mrs. Roger Woodman of Wayland, (92-71), and Mr. and Mrs. Stephen Whitcomb of The Country Club, (108-71).

Scott Hartz, Duxbury Yacht Club, with Lorraine Sheeran

Dr. and Mrs. J. Paul (Lorraine) Sheeran longtime members of Winchester Country Club

THE STONE CUP - MIXED FOURSOMES CHAMPIONSHIP

The MGA held the first mixed foursomes championship which was won by Glenna Collett and Clark Hodder at Weston Golf Club in 1924. Mr. and Mrs. Raynor M. Gardiner of Weston Golf Club, ardent fans of the mixed foursomes format, started the State Mixed Foursomes Championship. In 1925, they invited the WGAM to join them in running the tournament. In 1927, Katherine B. (Mrs. Edward C.) Stone from Oakley Country Club presented "The Club Pair Mixed Foursomes Championship Cup". Katherine Stone won the Association Championship in 1924 and she also served on the USGA Women's Committee. In 1957, the WGAM assumed full responsibility for this tournament.

Current Format: 18-hole mixed foursomes, alternate drives, match play for club pairs

The *inaugural tournament* was hosted by Weston Golf Club.
   Winners: Glenna Collett and Clark Hodder

The *Year 2000 tournament* was hosted by Taconic Golf Club.
   Winners: Susan Lemay & James Ruschioni of Oak Hill Country Club

There were two "SNOW" delays on the day of qualification and a "FROST" delay on the final day of play.

| Susan Lemay and James Ruschioni | *defeated* | Marion and William McInerney |
| Oak Hill Country Club | | Charles River Country Club |

THE STONE CUP - MIXED FOURSOMES CHAMPIONSHIP

Susan Dean, WGAM Vice President and husband, Charles, Foxboro Country Club
"What's a little snow - can't putt??"

Sally Foehl, WGAM President and husband, Allen,
Dedham Country and Polo Club
"Cold - who's cold? Just dress properly."

Gerry Baker holding plaque presented by Judy
Norton to Taconic Golf Club in appreciation of
hosting the Year 2000 Tournament.

MOTHER AND SON TOURNAMENT

Established in 1958 when the Women's Golf Association of Massachusetts assumed responsibility for this tournament which originated at Wellesley Country Club. The Association donated the Division I trophy in 1958 and the Division II trophy in 1982. The Division III trophy was donated by Pippy O'Connor in 1982.

Current Format: Divisions I and II: 18-hole foursomes, selected drive, alternate shots
Division III: 9-hole foursomes, selected drive, alternate shot

The *inaugural tournament* was hosted by the Dedham Country and Polo Club.
Winners: Mrs. John H. Nies and John, Jr.

The *Year 2000 tournament* was hosted by Tedesco Country Club.
Winners: Overall, Division I: Mary and Mike Gale of Tatnuck Country Club
Division II: Tami and Harry Bane of Kernwood Country Club
Division III: Robyn and Jack St. Clair of Brae Burn Country Club

Ann Grayson with her son, Jeff and
Nancy Black with her son, Paul

Suzanne Burgess
with her son, Jordan

Mary Gale with her sons, Dan (left), Joe and Mike

Kay Hood with
her son, Bill

MOTHER AND DAUGHTER TOURNAMENT

Established in 1997. Before that time, the Women's South Shore League allowed WGAM members to play in their Cris Eaton Mother and Daughter Tournament. As that tournament grew in size, the Women's South Shore League asked the WGAM to establish a tournament for WGAM members. In 1986, Nancy Black donated the Division I trophy which was won by Hannah and Loren Milhench. The WGAM purchased the Division II and III and overall trophies.

Current Format: Divisions I and II: 18-hole foursomes selected drive, alternate shot
 Division III: 9-hole foursomes selected drive, alternate shot

The _**inaugural tournament**_ was hosted by Newton Commonwealth Golf Club.
 Winners: Overall, Division I: Patricia and Courtney Marsh
 Division II: Nancy and Kristina Howard
 Division III: Sally and Samantha Hurwitz

The _**Year 2000 tournament**_ was hosted by Bayberry Hills Golf Course.
 Winners: Overall, Division I: Roberta Bolduc and Kathleen Schuster of Longmeadow Country Club
 Division II: Kathleen and Meghan O'Toole of The Ridge Club
 Division III: Anne Marie and Abigail Tobin of Bellevue Golf Club

Roberta Bolduc and her daughter,
Kathleen Schuster

Anne Marie Tobin and her daughter, Abigail

135

MOTHER AND DAUGHTER TOURNAMENT

*Megan Bearce with daughters,
Caitlin (left) and Hannah (right)*

Suzanne Burgess and her daughter, Cathy

*Virginia Laming (middle) with her daughter, Judi Krzynowek (right) and granddaughter, Darcy Krzynowek (left)
"Three Generations"*

DOLLY SULLIVAN TOURNAMENT

Dolly Sullivan

Established in 1982. The friends of Dolly Sullivan, recognizing her love of golf and her dedication to the Francis Ouimet Scholarship Fund, established the tournament as a tribute to this fine competitive golfer and teacher-coach. Since she was the niece and protégé of Francis Ouimet, her friends wished to establish a fund-raising event to benefit the Ouimet Scholarship Fund. The Tournament Committee members in that first year were Priscilla Bailey, Nancy Black, Jeanne-Marie Boylan, Selwyn Kudish and Pippy O'Connor. Dolly Sullivan Clocks, made by Bob O'Connor, Pippy's husband, are awarded to the low gross and low net champions to be held at their club for one year. In 1993, the WGAM Executive Board, in agreement with the Dolly Sullivan Committee, voted to include the Dolly Sullivan Tournament as one of its tournaments. It was recommended that a percentage of the proceeds go to the Ouimet Fund and the balance to the WGAM Junior Scholarship Fund. The recipient of this award is a high school senior who has participated in WGAM junior events and one who epitomizes the spirit and values that Dolly Sullivan exhibited. Currently, the Dolly Sullivan Tournament benefits the WGAM Junior Scholarship Fund, Inc., the WGAM/Dolly Sullivan Restricted Scholarship Fund, and the Francis Ouimet Scholarship Fund.

Current Format: 18-hole best ball of four, club teams

The *inaugural tournament* was hosted by the Country Club of Halifax.
  Winners: Gross: Barbara Quinn and Jeanne-Marie Boylan of
                        Wollaston Golf Club
              Net: Helen Gibbons and Anita Mauro of Marlboro
                        Country Club

The *Year 2000 tournament* returned to the Country Club of Halifax.
  Winners: Gross: Lisa Anderson, Lori Kelfer, Catherine Marquardt
                        and Noreen Trudel of Ferncroft Country Club
              Net: Maureen Brennan, Judy DiDomenico,
                        Sally Tuck, and Lauren Sexeny of Wellesley
                        Country Club

Friends of Dolly Sullivan
L-R: Pippy O'Connor,
Jeanne-Marie Boylan, Priscilla Bailey,
and Nancy Black

DOLLY SULLIVAN TOURNAMENT

Bridgette Palin
Recipient of the Year 2000
Dolly Sullivan Award

Year 2000 Gross Winners - Ferncroft Country Club
L-R: Noreen Trudel, Lori Kelfer, Lisa Anderson and
Catherine Marquardt, with WGAM past president,
Louise Mariani

Year 2000 Net Winners - Wellesley Country Club
L-R: Judy DiDomenico, Sally Tuck, Lauren Sexeny, and
Maureen Brennan

JUNIORS

"This year we lose many girls to that plague of all women AGE. Two of our girls, Jane Faxon and Janice Gannon, have been playing in our junior tournaments for the past nine years. They, with the others, have set an example that will be a challenge to all future junior golfers. I am proud to turn all these girls over to our Women's Association.

With the increased interest in developing junior programs within the clubs, I hope we will have many more playing juniors next year. If at any time you hear of a young girl interested in golf, please send me her name and address and I will be glad to contact her and see that she receives a schedule. I would also appreciate being notified if your club is sponsoring an open junior tournament. This would be added to our schedule and give the girls the added experience that is so important at this age.

I want to thank my very competent and efficient committee: Mrs. Robert Waldinger of Dedham; Miss Olive Nolan of Woodland; Mrs. Leo Arsenault of Segregansett, Miss Margaret Curtis, who never fails to appear to referee the 18-hole finals of our Junior Championship; and Mrs. Edward Baker who has the perfect qualities for a chaperone and the motherly instinct to see that the girls eat properly. Thank you all for your support and cooperation."

Eleanor George, Junior Chairman, 1961

Ellie George with Margaret Curtis

BEFORE THE PLAYOFF—Talking things over before their playoff at the Charles River Country Club, yesterday, are left to right: Mrs. Donald McCluskey, Worcester; Joanne Goodwin, Plymouth; Betty Dargie, and Mrs. Chapin Fay of Hillcrest. The Hillcrest members went on to capture low gross honors of the Senior-Junior Women's Scotch Championships in a five-hole playoff.

Margaret Ogg, 1939 Champion

Hillcrest Pair Golf Winners

A 12-foot downhill putt by Betty Dargie of Hillcrest on the fifth extra hole, gave her and her home club partner, Mrs. Chapin Fay, low gross honors in the W.G.A. senior-junior women's Scotch foursome competition at the Charles River Country Club, yesterday.

The Hillcrest combine posted an 80-76 to tie with Mrs. Donald McClusky, Worcester and Joanne Goodwin, Plymouth, who had an 80-78 to force the playoff. Pippy Rooney, Charles River, and Gretchen Dow, Dedham, took low net with an 81-69.

The summary:

Pippy Rooney, Charles River and Gretchen Dow, Dedham	81	69
Mrs. Paul Black, Marshfield and Patsy Parker, Myopia	89	73
Betsy Topham and Marcia Rand, Framingham	82	73
Mrs. William Verhage and Jane Woodruff, Needham	94	74
Mrs. Edward McAuliffe, Charles River and Suzanne Stebbins, Hatherly	85	75
Dorothy Sullivan, Marshfield and Anne Feely, Hatherly	84	75
Mrs. Fred Lockwood and Joan Igoe, Wellesley	94	76
Mrs. Chapin Fay and Betty Dargie, Hillcrest	80	76
Miss Blaisdell and Joan Barker, Green Hill	94	77
Margaret Frunaret, Brae Burn and Mary Werly, Duxbury	88	77
Beth Forte, Brae Burn and Candace White, Sherwood	92	78
Mrs. Walter Holland and Janice Meehan, Wollaston	98	78
Mrs. Donald McClusky, Worcester and Joanne Goodwin, Plymouth	80	78
Mrs. C. F. Bartholomew, Brae Burn and Dana Lombard, Weston	85	79
Mrs. Anne Sampson and Valerie Ketch, Merrimac Valley	93	79
Mrs. Walter Cosgrove, Wachusett and Ann Cosgrove, Green Hill	91	79
Mrs. Calvin Cook and Margaret Cook, Bass Rocks	101	80
Mrs. Lawrence Sargent, Wenham and Ellen Mahoney, Hatherly	97	80
Beatrice Beliveau, Oak Hill and Jury Rand, Framingham	97	81
Mrs. Maurice Simon and Anne Simon, Belmont	101	83
Mrs. James Parker, 2nd, and Jane Parker, Myopia	94	83
Mrs. William Burns and Regina Sullivan, Hatherly	108	83
Mrs. H. W. Scholl, Jr., Charles River and Gail McDonough, Hatherly	95	84
Mrs. Frederick H. T. Tarr, Jr. and Norman Harris, Rockport	103	85
Mrs. Francis King and Sheila Kallan, Hatherly	102	85
Mrs. Robert Williams and Betsy Ross, Needham	102	86
Mrs. Richard Hart and Eileen Deschamps, Wenham	92	86
Priscilla Bailey, Marshfield and Laura Chase, Hatherly	104	86
Mrs. Ray Heffernan, Wollaston, and Constance Molloy, Hatherly	99	86
Mrs. A. J. Seabury, Wenham, and Mary Crotty, Hatherly	107	87
Mrs. Warren Elwell, Bass Rocks, and Alice Cosgrove, Green Hill	106	87
Mrs. Michael Flynn and Mary Ellen Flynn, Salem	109	88
Mrs. Charles River, and Peg Byrnes, Hatherly	107	88
Mrs. Edward Bailey and Carol Brignini, Wellesley	101	90
Rosamond Chase, Charles River, and Sally Chase, Hatherly	109	90
Mrs. Shepard Williams, Brae Burn, and Donna GasHardi, Framingham	108	91
Mrs. Julian Soblen and Ann Morse, Belmont	115	93
Margaret Curtis, Essex, and June Faxon, Coonamesset	108	93
Miss Edwina Burns and Midge Connors, Hatherly	123	93
Miss Reilly and Gail Sullivan, Hatherly	116	96
Mrs. Lendon Snedeker and Jean Snedeker, The Country Club	116	97
Mrs. James Walter, Maynard, and Margaret Spenser, Fresh Pond	106	97
Mary Hargedon and Kitsy Cavanaugh, Hatherly	127	99

WGAM JUNIOR GIRLS' GOLF PROGRAM

Early on, Miss Margaret Curtis recognized the need to introduce young girls to golf and to give them opportunities to play so that they might develop into championship caliber players. She wrote to local golf professionals to obtain the names of some young girls who would be interested in playing in a Junior Championship. The first tournament was held in 1930 at Oakley Country Club with 10 young contestants. There was a qualifying round and three days of match play. Dorothy Hunter of Albermarle Country Club (Newton) won. Margaret's strategy seems to have been a good one. Dorothy Hunter went on to win the Association Championship four times. Since then, eleven other Junior Champions have gone on to win the Association Championship. In 1938, a separate Junior-Junior division for girls 13 years old and younger was added to the Junior Championship. Over the years, three Junior-Junior Champions (Dana Lombard, Noreen Friel, and Tracy Welch) have gone on to win the Junior Championship and later the Association Championship.

The WGAM Junior Golf Program continued to build through the 1940's and by the 1950's, junior girls' golf was going strong in Massachusetts. Besides the Junior and Junior-Junior Championships, the WGAM program included a Father-Daughter Tournament (now run annually by the Massachusetts Golf Association), a Junior Mixed Foursomes Tournament, and a Senior-Junior Foursomes Tournament. In 1955, the Massachusetts girls were invited to join the Junior Inter-City Matches between New York and Philadelphia. This event is the girls' equivalent of the Griscom Cup competition. In 1959, the Junior Tri-State Matches were established between Massachusetts, Connecticut and Rhode Island.

It was during the fifties that WGAM Junior golfers began to play on high school golf teams, normally the domain of the boys. A pioneer for this may have been Marcia Rand from Framingham who, in 1955, was the first girl to win a varsity letter at Framingham High School as a member of the Boys' golf team. Today, girls play on high school boys' teams; however, more schools now have girls' teams as well. Marcia was the 1953 WGAM Junior-Junior Champion.

Through the years, the WGAM roster of junior events has changed, with the focus shifting to include even younger girls. In 1976, the Mowatt Trophy was contested for the first time and, in 1988, a Mite division for girls ten and under was added to the Junior Championship. Each season, the WGAM sends information packets to junior girls. In 2000, there were a record number of 80 entrants for the Junior, Junior-Junior and Mite Championships.

The goal of the Junior Program remains the same as when it was initiated in 1930 – to introduce young girls to the game of golf, teach them to love it, and to develop into the best players that they can be.

WGAM JUNIOR COMMITTEE CHAIRMEN

Margaret Curtis	1930-37, 1942-49	Mrs. William P. Gibbons	1976
Mrs. Harold Kaler	1938-40	Jennifer Brown	1977
Mrs. John Crafts	1941	Fay DeRuvo	1978-81
Alice Jantzen	1950	Anne Marie Tobin	1982-85
Mrs. William Bell	1951-53	Jane Welch	1986-87
Ellie George	1954-56, 1959-66	Pippy O'Connor	1988-90
Mrs. Thomas Peterson	1957-58	Mary Wilkinson	1991-93
Mrs. A. Dixon Sykes	1967	Georgia Peirce	1994
Mrs. Allan Q. Mowatt	1968-70	Kathrine Ranere	1995-97
Mrs. Sanborn Vincent	1971-75, 1978	Anne Magee	1998-99
		Maureen Berry	2000

L-R: Pippy O'Connor, Mazzie Gogolak, Claire Nolan, Judy Freeman, Sally Croce, Anne Magee, Sue Rooney

THE WGAM JUNIOR CHAMPIONSHIPS

In 1930, Margaret Curtis became the crusader for Junior Golf in Massachusetts and created the WGAM Junior Championships. In 1938, a separate division for girls who were 13 years old and under was added and this was named the "Junior-Junior" Division. In an effort to create still more interest, the "Mite" Division for girls 10 and under was added in 1988. The winners of each division are awarded a silver tray to be held for one year. In 1998, the WGAM established a Most Improved Player Award in honor of Pippy O'Connor.

Current Format: Junior Division (ages 14 to 18) is 36-hole stroke play (18 holes each day); the Junior-Junior Division (ages 11 to 13) is 18-hole stroke play (9 holes each day); and the Mite Division (ages 10 and under) is 18 hole stroke play (9 holes each day).

The *inaugural Junior Championship* was hosted by Oakley Country Club. The winner was Dorothy Hunter.

The *Year 2000 Championships* were hosted by Bellevue Golf Club. The Junior Division winner was Stacey Wolejko with a score of 79-74-153; the Junior-Junior Division winner was Kimberly Donovan with a score of 42-42-84; the Mite Division winner was Brittany Wendell with a score of 34-37-71. The Pippy O'Connor Most Improved Player Award winners were Kerry Whalen in the Junior Division, Catherine Carey in the Junior-Junior Division; and Andrea O'Neil in the Mite Division.

CHAMPIONS

Junior

1930 Dorothy Hunter	1966 Pat O'Brien
1931 Dorothy Hunter	1967 Kathie Seymore
1932 Virginia Bascom	1968 Ruthann Donahue
1933 Norma Yeaton	1969 Ruthann Donahue
1934 Virginia Bascom	1970 Ruthann Donahue
1935 Sally Mosser	1971 Noreen Friel
1936 Alice Belanger	1972 Caren McGhee
1937 Alice Belanger	1973 Cindy Patterson
1938 Alice Belanger	1974 Monica Romano
1939 Margaret Ogg	1975 Leslie Greis
1940 Marcia Perin	1976 Mary Wilkinson
1941 Ann Fitzgibbons	1977 Mary Wilkinson
1942 Marcia Perin	1978 Sally Quinlan
1943-45 World War II	1979 Pamela Meany
1946 Gene O'Neil	1980 Pamela Meany
1947 Pippy Rooney	1981 Shiobhan Shields
1948 Mary Alice Reilly	1982 Marie Bonzagni
1949 Leila Fisher	1983 Loren Milhench
1950 Leila Fisher	1984 Beth O'Kelly
1951 Joanne Goodwin	1985 Loren Milhench
1952 Joanne Goodwin	1986 Tracy Welch
1953 Joanne Goodwin	1987 Jody Lombard
1954 Joanne Goodwin	1988 Carri Lee Wood
1955 Eileen Deschamps	1989 Tara Joy
1956 Dana Lombard	1990 Tara Joy
1957 Donna Woodcock	1991 Alexis Boyle
1958 Barbara Sanford	1992 Amanda Richards
1959 Janice Gannon	1993 Andrea Ackerman
1960 Jane Faxon	1994 Tamra Herman
1961 Betty Tobin	1995 Laura Torrisi
1962 Betty Tobin	1996 Laura Torrisi
1963 Mary Jo Ahlander	1997 Lisa Morgan
1964 Susan Pompeo	1998 Kelly Robb
1965 Mary Jo Ahlander	1999 Stacey Wolejko
	2000 Stacey Wolejko

Junior-Junior

1938 Emma Hooton	1970 Alice Kelly
1939 Mary Leavitt	1971 Amy Glibbons
1940 Ann Gerrish	1972 Debbie Hoffman
1941 Nancy Jones	1973 Amy Gibbons
1942 Not Held	1974 Susan Santucci
1943-45 World War II	1975 Robin Auger
1946 Edwina Burns	1976 Robin Auger
1947 Leila Fisher	1977 Kim Sylvaria
1948 Leila Fisher	1978 Susan Starsial
1949 Susan Inman	1979 Marcia Melone
1950 Ann Feeley	1980 Lynn Lumsden
1951 Dana Lombard	1981 Laura Flanagan
1952 Betty Dargie	1982 Kerry Lee O'Leary
1953 Marcia Rand	1983 Kerry Lee O'Leary
1954 Judy Rand	1984 Jody Lombard
1955 Judy Rand	1985 Tracy Welch
1956 Marie Pepin	1986 Molly Driscoll
1957 Jane Faxon	1987 Amanda Richards
1958 Mary Donahue	1988 Patsy Lyden
1959 Cathy Igoe	1989 Alexis Boyle
1960 Leslie Milliken	1990 Suzanne Ranere
1961 Leslie Milliken	1991 Andrea Ackerman
1962 Vicki Jenssen	1992 Andrea Ackerman
1963 Terry Cohen	1993 Colleen McDonnell
1964 Kathy Pompeo	1994 Colleen McDonnell
1965 Ruthann Donahue	1995 Bridgette Palin
1966 Ruthann Donahue	1996 Jill Blanchard
1967 Noreen Friel	1997 Jill Blanchard
1968 Carolynne Yurkstas	1998 Alison Walshe
1969 Carolynne Yurkstas	1999 Juli Wightman
	2000 Kimberly Donovan

Mite

1988 Joanne Padden
1989 Andrea Ackerman
1990 Colleen McDonnell
1991 Cancelled
1992 Emily Ryan
1993 Jean Hunnefeld
1994 –97 Cancelled
1998 Brittany Weddell
1999 Kimberly Donovan
2000 Brittany Weddell

Pippy O'Connor
Most Improved Player
Award:

Junior:
1998 Deidre Smith
1999 Lisa Morgan and
    Elizabeth Ann Shaw
2000 Kerry Whalen

Junior-Junior:
2000 Catherine Carey

Mite:
2000 Andrea O'Neil

JUNIOR CHAMPIONS

Maureen Berry, WGAM Junior Chairperson,
Kimberly Donovan, the
2000 Junior-Junior Champion

Stacey Wolejko
1999 and 2000 Junior Champion

Brittany Weddell
2000 Mite Champion

Pippy O'Connor presenting the
Most Improved Player Award
to Kerry Whalen

Mite and Junior-Junior winners at the 2000 Junior Championships
L-R: Shea Elizabeth Butler, Jaclyn Sweeney, Chelsea Curtis,
Kimberly Donovan, Brittany Weddell, Abigail Tobin, Kerry Harrigan, Becky Mangone

JUNIOR CHAMPIONS

Judy Rand (left), 1954 winner of the Junior-Junior Division, with Margaret Curtis and Jane Faxon, runner-up

Judy Rand went on to win the 1959 U.S. Girls' Junior Championship.

JUNIOR AND JUNIOR-JUNIOR COMPETITORS

L-R: Anne Cosgrove, Mary Hargraves, Gail McDonough, Kathleen Cosgrove, Margaret Spencer and Nancy Gibbons

Top Row L-R: Ann Feeley, Betty Dargie, Susan Connolly, Marcia Rand, Lynn Jamison and Alice Cosgrove;
Front Row L-R: Gail Sullivan, Ellen Mahoney, Kitty Cavanaugh and Martha Callahan

Junior Inter-City Team Matches

· The Junior Inter-City Team Matches began in 1955. The matches are between Boston, Philadelphia and New York City. Each team consists of six players.

**Current Format:** On the day preceding the matches, there is a best-ball sweepstakes event. Each team is made up of one player from each of the Associations. For the Junior Inter-City Team Matches, each Association is represented by a team of five players, plus an alternate; six three-ball matches are played.

The _**inaugural Junior Inter-City Team matches**_ in which Massachusetts participated were held at Greenwich Country Club, CT (part of the Metropolitan Association, New York). The winning team was Philadelphia.

The _**Year 2000 Junior Inter-City matches**_ were played at the Country Club of Fairfield (Fairfield, CT, member of the Metropolitan Association, New York). The results were: Philadelphia – 17 1/2 points, New York – 14 1/2 points and Boston – 13 points. The Boston team consisted of: Jillian Burtt, Liz Callery, Jessie Doyle, Liz Friel, Meghan O'Toole, Kelly Robb, and Meghan Sullivan.

The record through the years is as follows:

Boston	59, 60, 61, 62, 73, 74, 75, 77, 79, 80, 83, 87, 95, 96, 98, 99	16 Wins
New York	63, 64, 71 81, 82, 88, 90, 91, 97	9 Wins
Philadelphia	55, 56, 57, 58, 65, 66, 67, 68, 69, 70, 72, 78, 84, 85, 86, 89, 92, 93, 94, 00	20 Wins

The 1976 matches were not held.

BOSTON DOES HAVE A CHAMPION—Members of the Hub team that won the Inter-city championship yesterday are (from left), Barbara Policow, Plymouth; Marie Pepin, Happy Valley; Janice Gannon, Happy Valley; Cathy Igoe, Wellesley; Jane Faxon, Woods Hole; Jackie Keller, Plymouth.

Lead Boston in Inter-City Golf
Plymouth Girls Star

The Plymouth pair of Barbara Policow and Jackie Keller led the point contributors as the Boston entry won the junior girls' intercity golf matches for the second straight yesterday at the Woodland Golf Club.

Point tabulations for five Nassau System matches were: 20½ for Boston, 12½ for Philadelphia and 12 for New York. Boston defeated New York 10½-4½ and Philadelphia 10-5. The New York vs. Philadelphia duel was a 7½-7½ standoff.

MISS KELLER LOW SCORER FOR BOSTON

The 16-year-old Miss Policow, state junior finalist last year, swept all six points in her two matches, while her clubmate, Miss Keller, accounted for all but one half point in her two en-

counters. Barbara Policow was the day's only six point winner.

Miss Keller was the low scorer for the host group, carding a 45-41—86. Miss Policow returned a 42-47—89. Janice Gannon of Happy Valley had a score of 49-44—93. Jane Faxon of Woods Hole had a 54-48—102. The Lynn twosome of Miss Gannon and Miss Pepin won four points each.

Low scorer for the day was 16-year-old Mary Anne Doctor, the

leadoff player for the New York team. She toured the Auburndale layout in 41-43—84 to win all but one half a point in her three-way match with Jane Faxon and Sue Honeysett of Philadelphia. Miss Doctor is the daughter of Steve Doctor, well known New Jersey professional.

The prospects are good that Boston can win this inter-city competition again next year. Only Jackie Keller and Marie Pepin will be ineligible since they will have passed the 17-year age limit.

1996 Inter-City Team
L-R: Colleen McDonnell, Krissy McManus, Meghan Donoghue, Tami Herman, Laura Torrisi, Andrea Ackerman

1990 Inter-City Team
L-R: Tara Joy, Kristen McNamara, Jennifer Webster, Stephanie Poulin, Cathy Burgess, Molly Driscoll

JUNIOR TRI-STATE TEAM COMPETITION

The Junior Tri-State Team Competition began in 1959. The competition is between Connecticut, Massachusetts and Rhode Island.

Current Format: On the day preceding the matches, there is a best-ball sweepstakes event. Each team is made up of one player from each of the Associations. For the Tri-State Team Competition, each Association is represented by a team of five players, plus an alternate; six three-ball matches are played.

The *inaugural Junior Tri-State Team Competition* was held at New Haven Country Club, New Haven, CT. The winning team was Rhode Island.

The *Year 2000 Junior Tri-State Team Competition* was played at Crestwood Country Club in Rehoboth, MA (Rhode Island was the host state). The results were: Massachusetts – 97 points, Rhode Island – 90 points, and Connecticut – 84 points. The Massachusetts' team consisted of: Jillian Burtt, Elizabeth Friel, Meghan Mahoney, Caitlin Sullivan, Juli Wightman and Lauren Motyl.

The record through the years is as follows:

Massachusetts	1960, 1961, 1963, 1964, 1966-1970, 1972 –1982, 1984-1988, 2000	26 Wins
Rhode Island	1959, 1962, 1999	3 Wins
Connecticut	1965, 1983	2 Wins

The 1971 competition was cancelled due to inclement weather. The competition was not held from 1989 to 1998.

1970 winning Massachusetts Tri-State Team: L-R: Caren McGhee, Noreen Friel, Debbie Simourian, Nina Fiore, Terry Glass, and Ruth Ann Donahue

1999 Tri-State Team with Pippy O'Connor (far left) and Maureen Berry (far right). L-R: Stephanie Proto, Katherine Kuchefski, Lisa Morgan, Jillian Blanchard, Kelly Robb, Stacey Wolejko

THE MOWATT TROPHY

Established in 1971. The Trophy was donated by Doreen and Allen Mowatt.

Current Format: 18-hole four-ball, stroke play (juniors, ages 14 through 18). The Mowatt Trophy is awarded for the low gross score. In 1988, a scramble format was established for the Junior-Junior and Mite Divisions.

The *inaugural Mowatt Trophy* was hosted by Andover Country Club. The winners were Noreen Friel and Diane Fisher.

The *Year 2000 Mowatt Trophy* was held at Bear Hill Golf Club. The winners of the Junior Division were Caitlin Sullivan and Jillian Burtt with a score of 72. The winners of the Junior-Junior and Mite Division were Kerry Harrigan, Emily Mulcahy, Sarah Whitney, Abby Coyle with a score of 38.

WINNERS

1971 Noreen Friel & Diane Fisher	1986 Carri Lee Wood & Justine Richards (83)
1972 Caren McGhee & Marcia Veale	1987 Tracy Welch & Tara Johnson (78)
1973 Kathy Connor & Gayle Andrew	1988 Carri Lee Wood & Molly Driscoll (77)
1974 Leslie Greis & Marcia Veale	1989 Tara Joy & Ann Marie Carpenito (81)
1975 Amy Gibbons & Debbie Hoffman	1990 Stephanie Poulin & Jennifer Webster (82)
1976 Leslie Greis & Jane McCarthy	1991 Jennifer Machado & Laura Gilmore
1977 Amy Gibbons & Pam Meany	1992 Alexis Boyle & Laura Gilmore
1978 Marlene Susienka & Vanessa Costa	1993 Alexis Boyle & Laura Gilmore
1979 Vanessa Costa & Maureen Donovan (80)	1994 Kristen Infanger & Laura Torrisi (79)
1980 Pam Meany & Kathy Vendetti (69)	1995 Katie Cruise & Marissa Kulig (77)
1981 Mary Locke & Maria Bonzagni (74)	1996 Laura Torrisi & Andrea Ackerman (76)
1982 Debbie Davis & Sue Marion (73)	1997 Cancelled
1983 Heike Milhench & Loren Milhench (70)	1998 Colleen McDonnell & Bridgette Palin (70)
1984 Beth O'Kelly & Debbie O'Kelly (72)	1999 Kerry Whalen & Kathryn Kuchefski (72)
1985 Beth O'Kelly & Debbie O'Kelly (79)	2000 Caitlin Sullivan & Jillian Burtt (72)

*Caitlin Sullivan and
Jillian Burtt*

The Mowatt Scramble

*L-R: Kathryn Kuchefski,
Anne Magee, and Kerry Whalen*

W G A M

2000

WOMEN'S HANDICAP CLASSES
BY USGA HANDICAP INDEX

Class A	0-14.0
Class B	14.1-18.0
Class C	18.1-21.0
Class D	21.1-24.0
Class E	24.1-30.4

❖❖❖❖❖❖❖❖❖❖❖❖❖❖❖❖

JUNIOR TOURNAMENT SCHEDULE

Junior Inter-City Team Matches   CC Fairfield, CT
June 28-29 *(by invitation)*

Mowatt Trophy   Bear Hill GC
July 24

WGAM Junior Championships   Bellevue GC
August 7-8

Junior Tri-State Matches   Crestwood CC
August 22-23 *(by invitation)*

To be eligible for WGAM junior tournaments, participants shall be Massachusetts residents or have parents who are members of a Massachusetts club.
A handicap is not required.

JUNIOR CLASS: Any girl who has not reached her 19th birthday by the closing date of the tournament.
A competitor 18 years of age is eligible only if she has not yet begun her first semester of post-graduate education.

JUNIOR-JUNIOR CLASS: Any girl who is between the ages 11-13 years by the closing date of the tournament.

MITE CLASS: Any girl age 10 years and under by the closing date of the tournament.

For further information about membership, eligibility and tournaments contact:

Women's Golf Association of Massachusetts, Inc.
175 Highland Avenue
Needham, MA 02494
Telephone: 781-453-0555 Fax: 781-453-0827
Email:wgamass@usga.org Web Site:www.wgam.org

W G A M

2000
TOURNAMENT SCHEDULE

Event/Dates	Site/Classes
Spring Team matches	Participating Clubs
April 27, May 4, 11, 15, 18	All Classes
Eleanor W. Allen Bowl	Plymouth CC
May 25	C-D-E
Griscom Cup	Brae Burn CC
May 31, June 1-2	*(by invitation)*
Senior Championships	Kittansett Club
June 5, 6	A-B-C-D-E
Curtis Bowl	Myopia Hunt Club
June 12, 13	A-B-C-D-E
Class B & C Championships	Woodland GC
June 15	B-C
Cris Eaton Foursomes	Duxbury Yacht Club
June 26, 27	A-B-C-D-E
Class D & E Championships	Sterling CC
June 29	D-E
New England WGA	Sugarloaf USA, ME
July 11-13	0-17.4
Edith Noblit Baker Trophy	Cohasset GC
July 17-18	A-B
Association Championship	Oakley CC
July 25-28	Class A
Mother & Son	Tedesco CC
August 7, 8	0-30.4
Grace Keyes Cup	Charles River CC
August 14-15	Class A
Class "E" Better Ball	White Cliffs CC
August 21	Class E
Dolly Sullivan	CC of Halifax
August 22	A-B-C-D-E
Hannah D.Townshend Cup	Weston GC
August 28, 29	A-B
Mother & Daughter	Bayberry Hills GC
August 31	A-B-C-D-E
Sheeran Trophy	Winchester CC
September 12, 13, 14	0-24.0
Mildred Gardinor Prunaret Cup	Blue Hill CC
September 19-21	A-B
Endicott/Tri-State Matches	Orchards GC
September 26-28	0-17.0
Centennial Tournament	*Longmeadow CC*
October 2	*A-B-C-D-E*
Centennial Tournament	*Concord CC*
October 3	*A-B-C-D-E*
Eleanor I. LaBonte	Gardner GC
October 4, 5, 6	A-B-C-D
Stone Cup	Taconic GC
October 10-12	0-24.0

Year 2000 Members

Abbott, Marybeth
Abbruzzese, Judy
Abdow, Janet
Aberizk, Kathy
Accomando, Christine
Adams, Susan
Adams, Berit
Adams, Lois
Adamson, Helen
Adrien, Anne
Affleck, Jane
Agganis, Joyce
Agganis, L. Patricia
Agostini, Ann
Agostino, Sally
Ahlin, Dorothy
Ahlquist-Beach, Donna
Ahordini, Barbara
Ainsworth, Paula
Akers, Susan
Akey, Martha
Alberto, Barbara
Albiani, Carol
Aldo, Rose
Alexander, M.J.
Alexander, Marge
Allen, Erika
Alosky, Susan
Alsbach, Marijke
Altomare, Mary
Amanti, Norma
Ammerman, Karen
Anasoulis, Helen
Anderson, Margaret
Anderson, Lisa
Anderson, Carol
Anderson, Donna
Anderson, Karen
Anderson, Mary
Andrews, Marilyn
Anes, Jean
Annese, Debbie
Ansay, Patricia
Anthonson, Eleanor
Anzivino, Diana
Archambault, Suzanne

Arkush-Metsisto, Eevelyn
Armstead, Marjorie
Armstrong, Laurie
Armstrong, Carol
Arnold, Carol
Arnold, Sidney
Arnold, Betty
Aronson, Carole
Arsenault, Frances
Atherton, Gail
Atwood, Natalie
Austin, Debra
Avellone, Sandy
Aversa, Debbie
Ayotte, Nancy
Azzarito, Cecilia
Babin, Janice
Baden, Violeta
Badolato, Barbara
Bagdasarian, Nancy
Bagdon, Ellen
Bagley, Joan
Bagnall, Janis
Bailey, Priscilla
Bailey, Christina
Bain, Ann
Baker, Gerry
Baker, Lynley
Baker, Evelyn
Balboni, Jane
Baldwin, Lola
Baldwin, Moya
Ball, Julie
Balzarini, Judith
Bane, Tami
Banks, Marie
Banks, Jennifer
Baptista, Karen
Barbas, Esta
Barbookles, Janet
Bardhi, Susan
Baribeau, Dawn
Barns, Cathy
Baroncelli, Linda
Barr, Cynthia
Barres, Jill

Barrett, Nancy
Barrett, Betty
Barrie, Christine
Barron, Adele
Barry, Judith
Barry, Patricia
Barry, Jean
Bass, Linda
Batchelder, Pauline
Bateman, Deborah
Bateman, Barbara
Bates, Marcia
Bath, Janet
Battista, Josephine
Bearce, Megan
Beaty, Eleanor
Beaver, Marilyn
Beckerman, Nancy
Beckman, Marguerite
Bedard, Gloria
Bedard, Marie
Bedell, Kristin
Bedford, Ellen
Begley, Susan
Belanger, Linda
Belliveau, Leslie
Bena, Diane
Bender, Nancy
Bengis, Carol
Bengtsson, Kati
Bennett, Isabelle
Bennett, Mary
Bennett, Rosamond
Benoit, Lorraine
Benson, Diedre
Benson, Judith
Bentley, DeeDee
Berenson, Terry
Berg, Phyllis
Bergh, Constance
Bergholtz, Joyce
Berlo, Patricia
Berman, Mary
Berrett, Karen
Berrier, Joan
Berry, Maureen

Bersaw, Carolyn
Bertman, Isabel
Bessette, Janice
Beyer, Susie
Bianchi, Susan
Bianco, Susan
Bille, June
Bird, Maxine
Birdsall, Melinda
Birmingham, Karen
Bishop, Susan
Bishop, Valerie
Bissonnette, Anna
Black, Nancy
Blackman, Barbara
Blake, Deborah
Blakeley, Lucy
Blanchard, Pat
Blasdel, Maureen
Blaze, Barbara
Blethen-Coady, Jean
Blitz, Bernice
Blomstrom, Suzanne
Blomstrom, Joanne
Bloom, Terrie
Bloom, Deborah
Blum, Marjorie
Boday, Carolyn
Bodenmann, Linda
Boeing, Pat
Bohan, Jane
Bohman, Marita
Bohn, Mary Louise
Bolduc, Roberta
Bolduc, Ann
Bonneau, Jeanne
Bonnell, Patricia
Bonner, Sue
Bonnette, Brenda
Booma, Brenda
Boothman, Laura
Borden, Nicole
Borges, Jean
Borgschulte, Ann
Bornstein, Joyce
Borrelli, Carol

Bouchard, Linda
Boucher, Nancy
Boudreau, Cindi
Boudreau, Pam
Bourque, Kris
Bouvier, Joanne
Bovich, Mary Jo
Bowes, Margie
Bowler, Dorothy
Bownes, Alys
Boyd, Joan
Boylan, Jeanne-Marie
Boylan, Kathleen
Bradbury, Susan
Bradbury, Nancy
Bradbury, Maureen
Bradbury, Mary
Bradbury, Marie
Brady, Judith
Bragdon, Dorothy
Brainard, Susan
Braley, Dorothy
Braunhardt, Gloria
Braverman, Catherine
Bremner, Althea
Bremner, Dorothy
Brennan, Gloria
Brennan, Maureen
Brennan, Pat
Breslof, Phyllis
Briansky, Sue
Brickley, Nancy
Briggs, Catherine
Briggs, Jean
Briggs, Chris
Brindis, Anita
Brochetti, Sally
Brogan, Meg
Bronson, Wendy
Brooks, Toni
Brothers, Jane
Brothers, Elaine
Brown, Priscilla
Brown, Maura
Brown, Brett
Brown, Cathy

Brown, Marcia
Brown, Donna
Brown, Janet
Brown, Marjorie
Brown, Lynn Comandich
Brown, Janet
Brown, Cynthia
Brown, Diane
Browne, Melissa
Broyer, Christine
Bruno, Mary
Buchanan, Amy
Buck, Susan
Buckley, Kristen
Budash, Gail
Bue, Moira
Bugbee, Carol
Bulger, Helen
Bunch, Karen
Burgess, Catherine
Burgess, Mr. Jordan
Burgess, Carol
Burke, Mary Lou
Burnes, Barbara
Burns, Nancy
Burns, Stephanie
Burns, Carol
Burr, Diane
Burroughs, Rima
Burrows, Amanda
Bush, Winifred
Bush, Elaine
Butcher, Amy
Buter, Ann
Butera, Marie
Butler, Vera
Buttimer, Barb
Cadigan-Jones, Mary
Caefer, Beverly
Cahill, Carol
Cahners, Sue
Cain, Martha
Callahan, Joan
Callahan, Gretchen
Callander, Elise
Calvert, Gretchen
Cameron, Lanie
Campbell, Doris
Campbell, Jean
Campbell, Marilyn
Campbell, Patricia

Campbell, Constance
Caney, Chris
Cannalonga, Nancy
Cannon, Carol
Canon, Phyllis
Cantiani, Claire
Cappola, Dorothy
Carlson, Elna
Carlton, Nancy
Carmichael, Diane
Carney, Kathleen
Carr, Eve
Carr, Elizabeth
Carrazza, Suzie
Carroll, Janice
Carroll, Charlotte
Carter, Diane
Carter, Joan
Caruso, Beatrice
Cary, Eleanor
Case, Priscilla
Casner, Cynthia
Casper, Nancy
Cataldo, Diana
Catlin, Joanne
Catlin, Kylie
Catto, Bonnie
Caverly, Val
Ceddia, Maria
Cennerazzo, Tody
Ceppi, Jenny
Cesari, Lucille
Cesario, Lydia
Chabot, Debra
Chadwick, Nancy
Chaffee, Pauline
Chagnot, Nancy
Chamberlain, Mary
Chamberlain, Lesley
Chamberlain, Esther
Chapman, Ellen
Charlton, Beverly
Charron, Grace
Chatel, Wendy
Cheetham, Maryellen
Chefalo, Betty
Chenail, Lois
Chilton, Maude
Chisholm, Helen
Choi, Jenny
Christie, Barbara

Christmas, Maureen
Christoforo, Ruth
Chrusz, Dianne
Churchill, Kathleen
Ciani, Valborg
Ciccariello, Nina
Cies, Louise
Ciociolo, Margaret L.
Cirrone, Janet
Clarey, Carol
Clark, Mary Joe
Clark, Joan
Clarke, V. Barret
Clayson, Pam
Clear, Agnes
Cleaves, Barbara
Clifford, Charlene
Cluett, Maura
Coffill, Ruth
Coffin, Cynthia
Coffin, Karen
Cohoon, Jane
Colby, Sis
Colclough, Janet
Cole, Joan
Cole, Margery
Coleman, Janice
Coleman, Suzanne
Coleman, Patricia
Coleman, Marianne
Coletti, Myra
Colley, Helen
Collins, Joan
Collins, Nancy
Collins, Theresa
Colpitts, Bobbie
Conathan, Helen
Concannon, Patricia
Concannon, Nancy
Congdon, Christine
Conley, Cecilia
Conley, Catherine
Conlin, Virginia
Connaughton, Mary Z.
Connolly, Louise
Connolly, Kathleen
Connolly, JoAnne
Connor, Lynne
Connor, Suzanne
Connor, Mary
Connors, Joan

Connors, Nancy
Connors, Rosemarie
Conrad, Diane
Conroy, Marian
Cook, Susan
Cook, Cici
Cook, Marcia
Copeland, Barbara
Coras, Karen
Corcoran, Elizabeth
Corcoran, Carolyn
Corcoran, Barbara
Corcoran, Nancy
Cordner, Diana
Cornetta, Priscilla
Cornetta, Louise
Corradino, Joan
Corradino, Dolores
Corridan, Eleanor
Corrigan, Patty
Corson, Judy
Costa, Carolyn
Costa, Cassandra
Costello, Kathleen
Costello, Christine
Costello, Dianne
Cote, Jeanne
Cote, Pamela
Cote, Tracy
Cote, Luann
Cotton, Gina
Cotton, Betty
Coues, Phoebe
Coughlan, Sally
Coughlin, Christine
Coulstring, Louise
Courtemanche, Ellen
Couture, Henrietta
Cox, Michelle
Cox, Mazie
Cox, Martha
Coyle, Deirdre
Crabtree, Marybeth
Craig, Phyllis
Crane, Vicki
Crawford, Elizabeth
Crawford, Kristina
Croce, Sally
Crocker, Rebecca
Crockett, Joan
Croke, Doreen

Cronin, Mary
Crosby, Grace
Cross, Sandra
Crowell, Barbara
Crowley, Joan
Crowley, Mary Beth
Crowley, Marita
Crowley, Nancy
Cruise, Katie
Cumming, Ann
Cunniff, Christine
Cunningham, Eleaner
Cunningham, Rita
Curcio, Judy
Curran, Joellen
Curran, Cathie
Curry, Penny
Curtin, Susan
Curtis, Jane
Cusick, Barbara
Cussen, Betsy
Cutler, Sally
Cutler, Gertie
Dabney, Edith
DaCosta, Nancy
Dadoly, Constance
Daggett, Sue
D'Agostino, Sylvia
Daitch, Becky
Dalby, Helen
Dallamora, Robby
Dallamora-Mohan, Lea
Dallow, Lois
Damiani, Virginia
Daniels, Starr
Daniels, Margarett
D'Arrigo, Mary
Dauphinais, Agnes
Dautch, Patricia
Davenport, Jane
Davenport, Carol
David, Sandra
Davis, Abby
Davis, Sally
Davis, Maryann
Davis, Robyn
Davis, Kirsten
Davis, Katherine
Day, Laura
Day, Sandra
Deady, Kathleen

Deal, Barbara
Dean, Pamela
Dean, Susan
DeAngelis, Clare
DeCaire, Patricia
Deeb, Faye
Defeudis, Mary
DeGirolamo, Susan
Delany, Christine
Delgiacco, Mary
DeLuca, Susan
Demakes, Marill
Demars, Juneann
DeMatteo, Joan
DeMatteo, Judy
Dempsey, Donna
Dennis, Kelley
DePasquale, Eleanor
Derito, Margaret
DeRuvo, Fay
Desautels, Denise
DeSimone, Karen
DeVeer, Patricia
Devenis, Inga
Devereau, Doris
DeVilling, Trish
Devine, Mary Ann
DeVita, Sharon
Devlin, Donna
Devlin, Heidi
Diamond, Crystal
DiCarlo, Pam
Dickson, Margaret
Didio, Jacqueline
DiDomenico, Judy
Dieter, Susan
Dietrich, Alice
DiIorio, Ginger
Dings, Sandra
Dipesa, Carolyn
Dirlam, Maria
DiSangro, Pauline
DiVincenzo, Kathy
DiVincenzo, Sandra
Doane, Kathy
Doane, Marianne
Dobbins, Lynn
Dobson, Terry
Dobson, Anne
Doherty, Judith
Doherty, Sheryl

Doherty, Patricia
Doherty, Joean
Doherty, Ann
Doherty, Martha
Dolan, Kathleen
Dolan, Lynne
Dole, Johnnie
Donadio, Deborah
Donahue, Karen
Donahue, Ruth Ann
Donahue, Mary
Donahue, Rosella
Donahue, Susan
Donelin, Barbara
Doneski, Sue
Donlan, Kate
Donlon, Katherine
Donoghue, Jean
Donoghue, Meghan
Donoghue, Toni
Donohue, Marianne
Donohue, Mary
Donovan, Mary
Donovan, Carol
Donovan, Linda
Doran, Nancy
Dorian, Helene
Doucette, Gayle
Douglas, Nancy L.
Doyle, Donna
Doyle, Jae
Dragonas, Danise
Drew, I. Alice
Driscoll, Jeanne
Drohan, Jill
Drury, Dianne
Duane, Rita
DuBreuil, Sandra
Dudek, Jo
Dudley, Karen
Dufault, Karen
Duggan, Mary
DuGrenier, Mary
Duke, Vivi
Dunn, Eleanor
Dunn, Meredith
Durkes, Clement
Durkin, Elinor
Duryea, Linda
Duval, Betsyann
Duval, Lorraine

Duval, June
Dwyer, Beverly
Dwyer, Susan
Dyer, Molly
Eagan, Liz
Ebert, Leslie
Eddy, Jeanette
Eddy, Glenna
Ede, Roberta
Edmonds, Pat
Egan, Barbara
Ehlers, Mary
Ellis, Betty
Ellsworth, Pamela
Ellsworth, Gloria
ElMasry, Chris
Elmuts, Maggie
Embree, Joan
Emerson, Martha
Endlar, Alberta
England, Melissa
Eno, Susan
Enoksen, Arline
Eramo, Heidi
Esselen, Cathy
Essember, Carol
Estes, Virginia
Estridge, Marjorie
Eunson, Brenda
Evanoff, Molly
Evans, Kathleen
Evans, Susan
Evans, Sheila
Everett, Cherie
Everett, Florence
Everson, Constance
Everts, Elinor
Fagan, Dorothy
Fallon, Evelyn
Falzone, Eileen
Fardy, Diane
Farnham, June
Farrahar, Kathleen
Farrell, Muriel
Farrelly, Mariann
Farrington, Anne
Faulkner, Ruth
Faxon, Eileen
Feeney, Lorraine
Feeney, Jacqueline
Feld, Michele

Feldman, Linda
Fellows, Lorraine
Fenton, Anne
Fenton, Ruth
Fernandes, Frances
Ferney, Pat
Ferris, Nan
Ferry, Joanne
Ferry, Anne
Field, Martha
Field, Joanne
Field, Barbara
Fierra, Dorothy
Fifield, Elisabeth
Fillipovich, Angel
Fillmore, Setsuko
Filoon, Margaret
Filoramo, Anne
Finard, Andrea
Fink, Myra
Finkelstein, Bette
Finkelstein, Jill
Finlayson, Dorothy
Finlayson, Eleanor
Finley, Margot
Finne, Patricia
Finnerty, Wendy
Fish, Amy
Fish, Sally
Fisher, Cynthia
Fisher, Sue
Fishman, Clare
Fiste, Jane
Fitzgerald, Connie
Fitzgibbons, Ann
Fitzpatrick, Barbara
Fitzpatrick, Joan M.
Fitzwilliam, Donna
Flanigan, Patty
Fleming, Nancy
Flynn, Nancy Lea
Flynn, Florence
Flynn, Joanne
Flynn, Mary
Foehl, Sally
Foehl-Hemphill, Mace
Foley, Lois
Foley, Ann
Foley, Ellen
Folger, Barbara
Forbes, Dorothy

Forbes, Sarah
Foresman, Marcia
Forrest, Janice
Forsberg, Jane
Fortin, Beth
Fox, Janice
Frager, Camilla
Francoeur, Sharon
Frankel, Dori
Franklin, Arlene
Franzen, Leah
Franzino, Rita
Frazer, Judith
Freel, Patrice
Freeman, Janice
Freeman, Betsy
Freeman, Judith
Frem, Elizabeth
French, Karen
Frenette, Janet
Friar, Claire
Friend, Cynthia
Frizzell, Linda
Frost, Sue
Frost, Roberta
Frost, Joanne
Fuller, Sarah
Fuller, Janice
Fuller, Marty
Fuller, Joyce
Fulton, Dorothy
Gager, Patricia
Gagner, Janice
Gagner, Christine
Gagnon, Janet
Gahan, Catherine
Gailius, Lillian
Gaiotti, Annette
Gale, Mary
Gallagher, Madelyne
Gallagher, Melanie
Galligan, Natalie
Galligani, Lois
Gandolfo, Jo
Garabedian, Patricia
Garceau, Kathy
Gardner, Susan
Gardner, Susan
Gardner, Margaret
Garnett, Gabriella
Garrett, Theresa

Garvin, Joan
Gaudet, Flora
Geaney, Debra
Gebhardt, Elaine
Gedman, Sherry
Geehr, Olive
Gelb, Marilyn
Geldart, Terry
Geller-Petrini, Arlene
Gendron, Irene
Genser, Joan
Genser, Mira
Gent, Linda
George, Amalie Ann
Geraghty, Diane
Germaine, Martha
Gerson, Catherine
Gett, Lisbeth
Geupel, Ann
Giannelli, Maria
Giarrusso, Lisa
Gibney, Carol
Giffin, Lauri
Gilbert, Sheila
Gillen, Christina
Gillis, Louise
Gillis, Marlyn
Gillis, Karen
Glass, Lois
Glassburn, Donna
Gleason, Phyllis
Glor, Sarah
Glossa, Paula
Glovsky, Andrea
Gogolak, Mazzie
Gold, Penny
Goldberg, Pearl
Goldberg, Harriett
Golden, Mary
Goodwin, Jane
Gordon, Judy
Gordon, Emily
Gormley, Cindy
Gosselin, Marilda
Goulet, Linda
Goyette, June
Graham, Gail
Grannis, Jerri
Grant, Paula
Grant, Jansi
Gray, Marian

Grayson, Ann
Greehan, Janet
Greeley, Chapman
Green, Kimberlee
Green, Pamela
Green, Elizabeth
Greene, Marion
Greene, Phyllis
Greene, Marilyn
Greene, Davis
Greenfeld, Barbara
Greenhalgh, Barbara
Greenstein, Dorothy
Gregory, Caroline
Gregory, Sue
Griffin, Angela
Griffin, Priscilla
Gronoin, Marie
Groop, Priscilla
Gross, Rebecca
Grossman, Penny
Gruber, Ann Marie
Gryp, Lorraine
Guertin, Geraldine
Guillard, Katheleen
Guillette, Adrienne
Guiney, Mary Ellen
Gullotti, Mary
Gurry, Martha
Haag, Kathy
Haake, Susan
Haberman, Sally
Hackney, Jeanne
Hackstaff, Judith
Hadges, Dianne
Haffermehl, Helen
Hagl, Ann
Haight, Mary
Haley, Emily
Hall, Audrey
Hall, Fran
Hall, Margaret
Hall, Nancy
Hall, Janet
Haller, Marjorie
Hallet, Muriel
Halloran, Jean
Halloran, Karen
Halloran, Sharon
Hallowell, Robin
Hamel, Madi

Hamer, Diane
Hamilton, Patricia
Hamilton, Maureen
Hamilton, Nancy
Hamilton, Edie
Hammer, Ruth
Hanabury, Mary
Hanifin, Nancy
Hanlon, Lainey
Hanlon, Sarah
Hannaway, Florence
Harber, Diane
Hardiman, Yvette
Hardin, Sharon
Harding, Nancy
Harkins, Sheryll
Harmon, Lesley
Harrington, Beth
Harrington, Patricia
Harrington, Betty
Harrington, Diantha
Harris, Ellen
Harris, Nancy
Harris, Ellen
Harris, Carol
Harris, Deanie
Harris, Mary
Harrison, Deborah
Harrity, Dana
Hart, Karen
Harte, Jane
Hartley, Christiane
Hartman, Betty
Hartnett, Linda
Hartz, Linda
Harvey, Debbie
Harvey, Rosemary
Hasenfus, Laura
Hasiotis, Linda
Havern, Maureen
Havican, Conny
Hawthorne, Janice
Hay, Joan
Haydock, Candy
Hayes, Betsy
Hayes, Georgette
Hayes, Robin
Haynes, Sara
Hayward, Allyson
Hayward, Marsha
Hazard, Susan

Head, Patricia
Heald, Myrna
Healey, Priscilla
Heaney, Patricia
Heartfield, Marybeth
Hearty, Doris
Heath, Veronica
Heath, Candy
Hebert, Deborah
Heffernan, Kathleen
Heggie, Jane
Helinski, Carol
Henderson, Mimi Stefik
Hennessey, Jacqueline
Henry, Julie
Herlihy, Mary
Herscot, Carol Jane
Herter, Caroline
Hess, Emily
Hewins, Dorothy
Hewitt, Patricia
Hewitt, Emily
Hewitt, Sandra
Hexner, J. P.
Hickey, Maria
Hickey, Cathleen
Hickey, Margaret
Hickey, Pat
Hicks, Belinda
Hidden, Pat
Higgins, Cathy
Higgins, Lianne
Higgins, Roberta
Higgins, Mary
Hill, Judith
Hill, Abigail
Hill, Cecelia
Hill, Sharon
Hillberg, Paula
Hillis, Patrice
Hintlian, Becky
Hobbs, Mary
Hochberg, Judy
Hochman, Charlene
Hodgson, Catharine
Hoey, Maura
Hoffman, Joan
Hoffman, Molly
Hoffman, Robin
Holland, Claudia
Holmgren, Jeanne

Holt, Helen
Holt, Nancy
Hood, Kay
Hopkins, Marian
Hopkins, Beth
Hopper, Anne
Horgan, Linda
Horgan, Kathy
Horne, Georgia
Horwood, Barbara
Hostetter, Priscilla
Hotarek, Christine
Hovsepian, Nancy
Howard, Nancy
Howe, Elizabeth
Howlett, Mary
Hubbell, Carolyn
Huff, Karen
Hughes, Judith
Hughes, Edwina
Hughes, Carolyn
Hughes, Susan
Hulme, Pam
Hunsaker, Marcie
Hunt, Barbara
Hunt, Mary
Huntress, Betty
Hurd, Elizabeth
Hurley, Suzanne
Hurney, Elizabeth
Hurton, Mary Ellen
Hutcheson, Doris
Hutchins, Bette
Hynes, Jay
Hynes, Sandra
Incandela, Deborah
Ingemi, Nancy
Ingham, Elizabeth
Iris, Pat
Iselin, Sheila
Isenberg, Connie
Jackson, June
Jackson, Robin
Jacobs, Anne
Jaeger, Jane
Jaffarian, Kathryn
James, Nancy
Jamieson, Linda
Janes, Dorene
Janiak, Patricia

Jansen, Joyce
Janssen, Margriet
Jaslow, Susan
Jay, Emily
Jean, Delia
Jodice, Susanne
Johansson, Patricia
Johns, Jean
Johnson, Cindy
Johnson, Ginny
Johnson, Carol
Johnson, Pat
Johnson, Jane
Johnson, Michele
Johnson, Leta
Johnson, Sheila
Johnson, Gloria
Johnson, Gayle
Johnson, Tara
Johnston, Deborah
Johnston, Cynthia
Johnston, Jane
Jolles, Wendy
Jones, Donna
Jones, Rachel (Rae)
Jordan, Patti
Jordan, Sandra
Jortberg, Kathleen
Joseph, Karen
Joseph, Elaine
Joyce, Patricia
Joyce, Elaine
Judge, Trisha
Julier, Betsy
Juwa, Ava
Kabilian, May
Kade, Beulah-Ann
Kahl, Ada
Kahler, Ellen
Kaleta, Kathleen
Kaplan, Nancy
Kasses, Carol
Kaszanek, Brenda
Kates, Leslie Robinson
Kattar, Gayle
Kavanaugh, Patricia
Kaveney, Anne
Kay, Debbie
Kazanjian, Loralee
Keane, Patricia
Keane, Bernice

Keane, Carol
Keefe, Lois
Keefe, Judith
Keefe, Judy
Keeffe, Mary
Keegan, Patricia
Keigwin, Marilyn
Kelfer, Lori
Kelfer, Sandra
Kellar, Patricia
Kelleher, Fernande
Kelleher, Kathleen
Kelley, Marie
Kelly, Lori
Kelly, Janet
Kelly, Martha
Kelter, Mary
Kemp, Kendra
Kennedy, Ruth
Kennedy, Diane
Kennedy, Mary
Kennerly, Helen
Kenney, Mary
Kenny, Elizabeth
Keough, Helen
Kerkorian, Cynthia
Kerrigan, Marion
Kessel, Kathy
Kessler, Bette Ann
Ketcham, Mona
Kettendorf, Joan
Kew, Merle
Key, Elda
Kilcoyne, Joan
Kiley, Pam
Kilfoyle, Nancy
Killory, Lynne
Kim, Eun Joo
Kim, Hae Geun
Kim, Anne
Kimball, Joanne
King, Joyce
King, Paula
Kingsley, Christine
Kinnealey, Maura
Kinney, Georgette
Kirkham, Lois
Kirkwood, Gale
Kirwood, Barbara
Kitchen, Linda
Kleinas, Lauren James

Kleiner, Sandy
Klencheski, Beth
Klibansky, Maralyn
Klimann, Joan
Knight, Susan
Kochan, Sandra
Kompier, Diane
Konrad, Barbara
Koravos, Robin
Krake, Gretchen
Krasker, Jane
Kreeb, Marian
Krueger, Cheryl
Krzynowek, Judith
Kuhn, Deborah
Kunkel, Mary
Kusser, Susan
LaBonte, Joyce
LaBonte, Wendy
Labonte, Polly
Lacoste, Diane
Ladd, Lee
Ladner, Carol
Lafleur, Terry
LaFond, Patricia
LaGrasse, Karen
Lalley, Phyllis
Lamb, Janice
Lambert, Mary
Lander, Barbara
Landry, Kimberly
Lane, Brenda
Lane, Carol
Lange, Maggie
Langley, Rosemarie
Langley, Barbara
Lankau, Collette
Lannan, Kathleen
LaPrise, Alyx
Larson, Marge
Larson, Lucinda
Larson, Pat
Larson Hurley, Heidi
Lasher, Faye
Laskowski, Patricia
Latour, Janet
Lau, Joanna
Laurenza, Hazel
LaVallee, Barbara
Lavallee, Judith
LaVigne, Edith

Lavoie, Laurie
Lavoie, Jay Ann
le Gassick, Loren M.
Leader-Cramer, Nancy
Leary, Joyce
LeBlanc, Barbara
LeBlanc, Doris
LeBlanc, Betty
LeBlanc, Anne
Leccese, Anita
LeClair, Joyce
Leddin, NaThelle
Ledger, Betty
Leerer, Judy
Leger, Pam
Legere, Zita
Lehmberg, Janice
Leland, Rebecca
Lemay, Susan
Lemelin, Rona
Lenhart, Vikki
Leonard, Linda
Leonard, Helen
Leone, Donna
Leone, Frances
Lerch, Carol
Leritz, Ellen
Lesse, Tobi
Lester, Collette
Leventhal, Sara
LeVert, Penny
Levin, Marjorie
Levine, Marion
Levy, Erma
Lewin, Ellen
Lewis, Valerie
Lewis, Edith
Lexander, Donna
Libby, Bette Ann
Libin, Sara
Libin, Carol
Liddy, Molly
Lilly, Kristen
Linehan, Nicky
Linnehan, Stephanie
Linsky, Elaine
Litchfield, Irene
Locke, Penny
Locke, Barbara
Lockwood, Marie
Lombara, Julie

Lonergan, Marion
Long, Kathy
Looney, Constance
Lorentzen, Mary Ann
Loring, Hollis
Loring, Vicki
Loud, Christine
Lowe, Joan
Lublin, Sheri
Lucardi, Eileen
Lucas, Linda
Lucci, Dianne
Luccini, Kathy
Lund, Judith
Lundin, Margaret
Lundstedt, Ann
Lynam, Colleen
Lynch, Christine
Lynch, Carol
Lynch, Genevieve
Lynch, Kathryn
Lyons, Pat
Macallister, Susan
Macallister, Jan
Macaulay, Betty
MacInnis, Joanne
MacKenzie, Darlene
Mackey, Winnie
Mackin, Susan
MacMillan, Mary
MacNeill, Nancy
MacPherson, Joan
Maddox, Patricia
Madore, Carmen
Magee, Anne
Magee, Marilyn
Magill, Rachel
Maguire, Julie Anne
Mahan, Elizabeth
Mahan, Kelly
Mahar, Carol
Maher, Pat
Mahoney, Barbara
Mahoney, Eleanor
Mahoney, Bette
Mahoney, Meghan
Mahoney, Ruth
Mailloux, Deborah
Main, Mona
Malchodi, Joy
Mallaghan, Becky

Mallett, Debbi
Maloney, Celeste
Mandragouras, Ana
Manley, Nancy
Manning, Lucille
Mansbach, Pamela
Manzi, Donna
Marandett, Nancy
Marchioni, Esther
Marcos, Karen
Marengi, Mary
Marglous, Idele
Mariani, H. Louise
Marion, Jill
Markin, Susan
Marks, Mary Hurley
Marlio, Muffy
Marotta, Judith
Marotta, Fran
Marquardt, Catherine
Marsh, Patricia
Martignetti, Terry
Martin, Nance
Martinelli, Susan
Martinho, Jean
Martini, Katherine
Martino, Roseanne
Martis, Peggy
Martorano, Judith
Masland, Jean
Mason, Janet
Massad, Dorothy
Mather, Carol
Matthes, Ursula
May, Barbara
May, Norine
May, Nancy
McAuliffe, Gene
McAvoy, Mary
McCabe, Elizabeth
McCafferty, Patricia
McCance, Allison
McCann, Roberta
McCarthy, Linda
McCarthy, Patricia
McCarthy, Claudia
McCarthy, Joyce
McCarthy, Marie
McCarthy, Lorraine
McCarthy, Ginny
McClintock, Stella

McCloskey, Dianne
McClure, Jean
McClutchy, Catherine
McCombe, Peg
McConnell, Jeanne
McCormick, Susan
McCoy, Carolyn
McCrevan, Deloris
McCutcheon, Janet
McDavitt, Linda
McDermott, Cathy
McDermott, Loretta
McDermott, Kelly
McDermott, Sharon
McDonald, Kelly
McDonald, Patricia
McDonald, Laurajean
McDonnell, Jean
McDonnell, Colleen
McDonough, Mary
McDonough, Kay
McDowell, Kimberly
McEvoy, Donna
McGee, Anne
McGinn, Phyllis
McGinn, Suzanne
McGinnes, Louise
McGirr, Harriet
McGlynn, Kerri
McGovern, Anne
McGuire, Sheila
McHale, Carolyn
McHugh, Marie
McInerney, Marion
McInnis, Ellen
McKenna, Kathleen
McKissock, Ann
McLain, Laura
McLaughlin, Debbie
McLean, Candace
McMahon, Nancy
McManus, Nancy
McManus, Barbara
McMenimon, Catherine
McNamara, Mary
McNamara, Ruth
McNamara, Joanne
McNeice, Laurie
McNutt, Patricia
McParland, Beth
McPhail, Mary

McPherson, Colleen
McQuade, Angela
McQueen, Catherine
McSheffrey, Lauren
McSweeney, Kathleen
Meehan, A.J.
Meek, Libby
Mehlman, Lila
Melchionda, Jane
Melchionno, Patricia
Mello, Lori
Melly, Janice
Merrell, Julie
Mersch, Jeanne
Messina, Paula
Metcalf, Alison
Metras, Sheri
Meyer, Heidi
Micciche, Marilyn
Michaels, Mary
Michaud, Deborah
Michel, Betsy
Mikkila, June
Millard, Betsy
Miller, Michele
Miller, Kristin Anderson
Miller, Patricia
Miller, Shirley
Miller, Marilyn
Mills, Lorraine
Mills, Kiyoko
Milosh, Bata
Mineck, Virginia
Minton, Rita
Mirabile, Arline
Mirbach, Julie
Mitchell, Martha
Mitchell, Joy
Mitchell, Emily
Mitchell, Marcia
Mitman, Mildred
Molesworth, Phyllis
Monaghan, Jean
Monahan, Anne
Monahan, Joanne
Monahan, Jill
Monahan, Cynthia
Mongeau, G. Elaine
Mongeon, Diane
Monies, Frances
Montminy, Sheila

Mooney, Joan
Mooney, Mary Ellen
Moran, Mary
Moran, Janet
Moran, Brenda
Morawiec, Tiffany
Morgan, Laura
Morgan, Rosie
Morgan, Dottie
Morgan, Anne
Morgan, Lisa
Morin, Joan
Morris, Kathleen
Morrow, Jane
Morse, Caroline
Morton, Cindy
Mosher, Carole
Moss, Ada
Mosse, Judith
Motta, Judith
Moulton, Carolyn
Mucciarone, Pauline
Mulford, Janet
Mullahy, Diane
Mullen, Helen
Mullin, Katherine
Mullin, Kathleen
Mulroy, Marian
Murphy, Margaret
Murphy, Jeanne
Murphy, Anita
Murphy, June
Murphy, Debra
Murphy, Nancy
Murphy, Dale
Murphy, Jeanne
Murphy, Nancy
Murray, Patricia
Murray, Prudence
Musche, Susan
Muzzioli, Janet
Nagle, Kathy
Najarian, Heather
Najarian, Denise
Nardone, Fay
Nartowt, Joan
Nassau, Chloe
Nasson, Harriet
Nedoroscik, Connie
Neher, Molly
Neher, Dawn

Neill, Priscilla
Neilson, Anne
Neipris, Debbie
Nelson, Barbara
Nelson, Suzanne
Nelson, Patricia
Nessralla, Diane
Nesvet, Wendy
Neuger, Carol
Nevils, Barbara
New, Laura
Newsome, Karen
Neylon, Mary Ellen
Niblet, Pauline
Nichols, Beth
Nicholson, Mary
Nicolazzo, Susanne
Nicoll, Kathy
Nietsche, Jennifer
Nightingale, Elizabeth
Nigro, Althea
Nitikman, Nancy
Nixon, Anita
Noecker, Carlee
Nogelo, Gerry
Nolan, Claire
Nolan, Olive
Noonan, Joan
Norrman, Donna
Northrop, Pamela
Norton, Bette
Norton, Judith
Norton, Beth
Norton, Nancy
Notman, Deborah
Novak, Janice
Nunes, Robin
Nurczynski, Betsy
Nurse, Susan
Ober, Kimberly
Oberbillig, J. Lynn
O'Brien, Barbara
O'Brien, Mary
O'Brien, Faye
O'Brien, Karrell
O'Brien, Maureen
O'Brien, Clare
O'Brien, Joanne
O'Callaghan, Clare
Ochs, Jane
O'Connell, Linda

O'Connor, Donna
O'Connor, Jean
O'Connor, Susan
O'Connor, Edith
O'Connor, Pippy
O'Connor, Sally
O'Connor, Ann
O'Day, Sally
O'Donnell, Carolyn
O'Duggan, Deborah
Oehme, Gretchen
Oettinger, Marlys
Offringa, Gail Thomas
O'Grady, Patrice
O'Grady, Virginia
O'Halloran, Anne
Ohanian, Lu Ann
O'Keeffe, Darlene
Oldfield, Audrey
O'Leary, Jackie
Oliveira, Charlotte
Olmsted, Mary
Olmsted, Dianne
Olson, Patricia
Olson, Claire
Olson, Susan
Olthof, Gerrie
O'Neal, Louise
O'Neil, Pamela
O'Neil, Carol
O'Neil, Anne
O'Neill, Diane
O'Neill, Lya
Orlando, Lorette
Orlen, Laura
Ormon, Joan
Orr, Peggy
Osganian, Nora
Oshry, Eleanor
Ostman, Joyce
Ostrander, Patricia
Ota, Diane
O'Toole, Nancy
O'Toole, Kathleen
O'Toole, Meghan
Pacella, Carolyn
Padden, Patricia
Page, Valerie
Pagliarulo, Donna
Paharik, Gloria
Palazzo, Gloria

Palci, Linda
Palin, Bridgette
Palladino, Margaret
Palmer, Diane
Palmer, Patricia
Palmer, Suzanne
Palmer, Sherry
Panaccione, Jacqueline
Panicucci, Jane
Pannoni, Paula
Pantos, Maureen
Pappathanasi, Kym
Pare, Mary
Parent, Peggy
Paris, Roberta
Paris, Brenda
Parker, Jane
Parks, Marian
Parody, Alita
Parr, Ruth
Parrott, Hilda
Parrow, Sandra
Parziale, Laura
Pasquale, Joan
Patrick, Marty
Patrick, Megan
Patten, Nancy
Patten, Debra
Pavlas, Cathy
Pawloski, Kathleen
Payne, Leslie
Pearl, Sandra
Pearson, Virginia
Pearson, Alexandra
Peirce, Georgia
Pennington, Nuala
Pereira, Cynthia
Perkins, Claire
Perkins, Kathleen
Perkins, Barbara
Perneta, Pat
Perreault, Kathy
Perry, Martha
Perry, Stephanie
Perry, Gayle
Perry, Karen
Peters, Claudia
Peterson, Susan
Peterson, Jayne
Peterson, Nancy
Peterson, Janet

Petrie, Jane
Petrin, Yolande
Petrozzi, Linda
Phelan, Mary
Philipp, Joan
Phillimore, Coleen
Picciandra, Joan
Picken, Lewel
Pierce, Janet
Pierce, Allon
Pierce, Diane
Piercey, Judy
Pierpont, Leslie
Pignato, Patricia
Piken, Sally
Pisani, Jeanne
Pittenger, Lee
Pitts, Karen
Plote, Zena
Plungis, Kathleen
Podesta, Anita
Podgorski, Karen
Pohl, Andrea
Pola, Velia
Poland, Nancy
Pontoppidan, Myanna
Poor, Carol
Pope, Jinny
Pope, Mary
Popp, Cheryl
Porazzo, Marie
Porkola, Janice
Porter, Weslie
Potter, Lee
Potter, Penelope
Powell, Suzanne
Powers, Joan
Powers, Jean
Powers, Yuki
Prayzner, Cynthia
Preston, Joan
Preston, Kathleen O'Leary
Pringle, Julia
Prisco, Laura
Procter, Lisa
Putnam, Christine
Pynn, Donna
Quinn, Madeline
Quinn, Judith
Quinn, Barbara
Quinn, Joyce

Radochia, Sandra
Rafuse, Bonnie
Raker, Heather
Ramini, Maureen
Ramsey, Joanne
Randall, Romaine
Randall, Nancy
Randazza, Mickey
Randle, Ruth
Ranere, Kathrine
Rapa, Donna
Rapoza, Angelica
Rappaport, Phyllis
Rappoli, Carol
Rath, Sandra
Rautiola, Lois
Raymond, Anna
Raynor, Barbara
Recht, Lindy
Redquest, Larraine
Regan, Rhonda
Regan, Linda
Regan, Nancy
Regan, Gail
Regis, Kathy
Reid, Dorothy
Reid, Virginia
Reidy, Jean
Reidy, Jane
Reilly, Lola
Reilly, Katherine
Reilly, Penelope
Rennie, Carol
Replogle, Jeanne
Reynolds, Cass
Rhieu, Ann
Rice, Jody
Rice, Mary
Richard, Irene
Richards, Colleen
Richards, Claudette
Richards, Pamela
Richardson, Karen
Richardson, Diana
Rielly, Nancy
Riley, Terry
Riley, Marilyn
Riley, Margie
Riley, Marybeth
Riordan, Susan
Ritchie, Marge

Robb, Kelly
Robbins, Lucy
Robert, Earlene
Roberts, Abigail
Roberts, Madeline
Roberts, Candy
Roberts, Alice
Robey, Allie
Robichaud, Sandra
Robinson, Beth
Robinson, Carole
Robinson, Audrey
Rockwell, Lois
Rockwell, Sheila
Rodier, Loretta
Rodricks, Dianne
Roeder, Jill
Rogde, Isabelle
Roger, Eileen
Rogerson, Kye
Rogowski, Sally
Romano, Elisa
Romsavich, Deanna
Ronty, Natalie
Rooney, Susan
Root, Margaret
Rorke, Faye
Rosa, Jill
Rose, Patricia
Rose, Merle
Rosenberg, Gail
Rosenberg, Jane
Rosenberry, Mary Ellen
Rosenfield, Patricia
Rosenthal, Judith
Ross, Jo Ann
Rossi, Julie
Rost, Jane
Roth, Linda
Rothbard, Elise
Rowell, Leslie
Roy, Phyllis
Roy, Lynnette
Royer, Denise
Rubenstein, Carolyn
Rubin, Marian
Rubinstein, Lisa
Ruggeri, Carol
Rullmann, Shirley
Russo, Andrea
Russo, Letty

Ryan, Kathryn
Ryan, Maire
Ryan, Karen
Ryan, Molly
Ryan, Karen
Ryland, Marjorie
Rytuba, Lucy
Ryus, Mary Louise
Sabbag, Brenda
Sabella, Mary
Safner, Isadora
Sager, Lynne
Sakelarios, Susan
Sakowicz, Geri
Salamone, Cynthia
Salmon, Marcia
Salome, Christine
Sampou, Elsa
Sampson, Ann
Samuels, Clarissa
Sandreuter, Nancy
Santamaria, Eva
Santin, F. Virginia
Santoro, Joy
Santos, Janet
Santry, Anni
Sarkisian, Beatrice
Satin, Nancy
Saunders, Geralyn
Savage, Maureen
Savage, Carolyn
Savageau, Regina
Scangas, Pamela
Schaefer, Joan
Schaefer, Lori
Schaffer, Sally
Schara, Joan
Schavone, Beverly
Scheff, Doris
Scheffer, Rosalind
Scherer-Dodds, Denise
Schikorra, Irma
Schiller, Leslie
Schipani, Paulette
Schissel, Jean
Schmidt, Enid
Schmitt, Anne
Schofield, Joan
Schreck, Bonneta
Schug, Helen
Schumann, Paula

Schuster, Kathleen
Schwandt, Cheri
Schwartz, Penny
Scoon, Kristine
Scott, Karen
Scullane, Shirley
Scully, Elizabeth
Seale, Martha
Sealund, Eileen
Sears, Gihon
Segal, Donna
Seguer, Elaine
Sellew, Helen
Semple, Laura
Serino, June
Settles, Shyla
Sexeny, Lauren
Sgarzi, Donna
Shaak, Jean
Shann, Mary
Shaw, Barbara
Shaw, Mary Lou
Shea, Gertrude
Shea, Nancy Ann
Shea, Laura
Shea, Paula
Shean, Helen
Sheehan, Patricia
Sheeran, Lorraine
Sheffield, Mary
Shelton, Patricia
Shepherd, Joyce
Sherbrooke, Kathleen
Sherman, Joan
Sherman, Susan
Sherwood, Sumiko
Shoer, Faith
Shotwell, Jane
Shrinsky, Ronnie
Shulman, Audrey
Siegel, Sheri
Siegel, Sherry
Siegel, Sharon
Sigda, Susan
Silva, Judith
Silver, Marge
Silverman, Jerilyn
Silverstein, Deborah
Silviera, Rita
Simmons, Jean
Simonds, Judy

Simonds, Louise
Simpson, Patricia
Singleton, Priscilla
Sirois, Sheila
Sizemore, Jo
Skerry, Marianne
Slade, Judith
Slawsby, Gail
Slayton, Faye
Small, Joan
Smiley, Roberta
Smith, Anne Marie
Smith, Janice
Smith, Margaret
Smith, Holly
Smoragiewicz, Margaret
Snelders, Joanne
Snickenberger, Wendy
Snider, Roberta
Snow, Jane
Snow, Lee
Snowden, Irene
Snyder, Joanne
Soboczinski, Carol
Soja, Marsha
Solomita, Mary
Solomon, Karen
Soltesz, Margaret
Soltys, Mary Ann
Sommers, Kathryn
Sopp, Joan
Sousa, Sharon
Southworth, Ann
Souza, Judith
Spatharos, Mary Ann
Spaulding, Susan
Speers, Martha
Spinale, Lisa
Spinelli, Marilyn
Spiro, Dorothea
Spring, Deborah
Squillante, JoAnn
St.Clair, Robyn
St.Pierre, Kerry
Stackhouse, Sheila
Staniar, Mary
Stanton, Annmarie
Stark, Gloria
Starr, Elizabeth
Stebbins, Claire
Steele, Linda

Stein, Rhonda
Stella, Barbara
Stevens, Kathie
Stewart, Ruth
Stewart, Bonnie
Stewart, Nancy
Stikeleather, Linda
Stocks, Rosemary
Stoddard, Deborah
Stoller, Roberta
Stone, Laurie
Storey, Kathleen
Storey, Nancy
Stout, Ellen
Stowe, Lonnie
Straight, Maryalyce
Strand, Sylvia
Stringer, Susan
Strzetelski, Joyce
Sturgis, Katharine
Sugrue, Jane
Sullivan, Louise
Sullivan, Ellen
Sullivan, Caitlin
Sullivan, Marilyn
Sullivan, Ellen
Sullivan, Maureen
Sullivan, Dolores
Sullivan, Catherine
Sullivan, Barbara
Sullivan, Donna
Summit, Sheila
Suprenant, Linda
Surette, Jeanette
Sutherland, Joanne
Swaim, Patricia
Swaim, Jean
Swanson, Ingrid
Sweeney, Mary
Swindell, Jean
Swirsky, Renee
Sydlowski, Paula
Sylvia, Yvonne
Szymczak, Jo-Ann
Taffe, Andrea
Taggart, Theodora
Tague, Sara
Taicher, Nancy
Tak, Sue
Takahashi, Kyoko
Talbot, Marcia

Talbot, Jane
Tangherlini, Victoria
Tarullo, Maria
Tassinari, Ellen
Taylor, Belle
Taylor, Dianne M.
Taylor, D.C.
Tedeschi, Kate
Tedford, Andrea
Temple, Catherine (Cathy)
Terrasi, Marita
Tholander, Marion
Thomas, Georgia
Thomas, Hilary
Thomas, Dorothy
Thompson, Jessica
Thompson, Patty
Thompson, Lynda
Thompson, Gail
Thompson, Irene
Thompson, Jane (Moore)
Thomson, Virginia
Thorne, Libby
Thorner, Barbara
Thornton, Deborah
Thrasher, Jo Ann
Tiano, Kim
Tibbetts, Maggie
Tierney-Curry, Sheila
Tietje, Eleanor
Tillett, Sandra Rae
Tobey, Barbara
Tobin, Anne Marie
Todesco, Mary Joan
Tomasello, Sandra (Place)
Toomey, Jeanne
Topham, Pat
Torres, Roberta
Torrisi, Laura
Torrisi, Maria
Tosi, Beatrice
Tower, Valerie
Towle, Fran
Towler, Judith
Tracy, Constance
Trainor, Christine
Trainor, Kathleen
Trask, Julie
Traverse, Maureen
Treannie, Beverly
Tremallo, Susan

Tribou, Mary
Tricomi, Dianne
Tripp, Lynda
Troy, Mary Lynn
Trubiano, Lisa
Trudel, Noreen
Trussell, Leea
Tuck, Sally
Tucker, Nancy
Tully, Sally
Tully, Melissa
Tutun, Margot
Twombly, Judith
Tyrrell, Phyllis
Uchin, Phyllis
Uihlein, Tina
Ungerer, Dorothy
Vale, Nancy
Valentini, Sarah
Vana, Debbie
Vance, Janice
Vanslette, Estelle
Varner, Teresa
Varney, Linda
Varnum, Martha
Veale, Marcia
Veator, Christine
Veld, Priscilla
Veleno, Kathleen
Venning, Kay
Verani, Marguerite
Vergobbe, Terry
Vernaglia, Carolyn

Vernet, Ann
Vernon, Abigail
Vesey, Michele
Videtto, Barbara
Viger, Marlene
Vinson, Kathleen
Vogel, Helen
Vogel, Mabel
Vontzalides, Georgia
Waddleton, Lauria
Wagman, Gail
Wahlrab, Joyce
Wailes, Lynn
Walker, Ellen
Walkey, Joan
Wall, Sarah (Tee)
Wall, Mary Ann
Wallace, Leone
Wallace, Gigi
Wallace, Robin
Walsh, Marcia
Walsh, Maureen
Walsh, Beatrice
Walsh, Karen
Walsh, Bonnie
Walsh, Donna
Walsh-Gould, Deborah
Walter, Nancy
Waniga, Jan
Wanless, Lou
Wappel, Teresa
Ward, Judith
Ward, Mary Ann

Ward, Mary
Warner, Elizabeth
Warshaver, Shari
Watson, Pauline
Watson, Dorothy
Watson, Debra
Wayne, Marilyn
Webster, Ann
Weidler, Janet
Weiner, Judy
Weinshel, Enid
Weiss, Sarah
Weiss, Marnee
Welch, Tracy
Welch, Jane
Welch, Kathleen
Welch, Mary Jane
Weller, Gloria
Wells, Patricia
Wentworth, Peri
Wenzel, Evelyn
Werner, Judie
West, Patricia
Wester, Caroline
Westgate, Beatrice
Whalen, Kerry
Wheeler, Sharon
Wheeler, Karen
Wheeler, Sylvia
White, Elizabeth
White, Eileen
White, Margot
White, Tammy

White, Lois
White, Sandra
Whitman, Estelle
Whitman, Winifred
Whitman, Sally
Whitney, Sharon
Whitney, Patty
Whitridge, Sally
Whitworth, Kimberly
Wieland, Louise
Wieners, Carla
Wigglesworth, Penny
Wilder, Christina
Wildes, Joanne
Willard, Dot
Williams, Karen
Williams, Karen
Wills, Susan
Willwerth, Julie
Wilson, Jane
Wilson, Mary
Windhol, Anne
Windle, Fabia
Winfrey, Chris
Winn, Elizabeth
Winsor, Ruth
Winters, Pam
Wirta, Linda
Witt, Betsy
Witty, Arlene
Wojtkowski, Linda
Wolbarsht, Kasey
Wolfe, Lynda

Wood, Kathy
Wood, Jan
Woodworth, Bess
Woolley, Patricia
Worcester, Robin
Worden, Margaret
Wright, Ellie
Wright, Karen
Wrightson, Lois
Wunder, Nancy
Wykoff, Faith
Wykoff, Jane
Wyman, Diana
Wynne, Helen
Yadisernia, Janice
Yanofsky, Pamela
Yanofsky, Marcia
Yellen, Ronni
Yellope, Susan
Young, Jeanne
Young, Eugenia
Young, Joan
Yozell, Barbara
Yule, Lee
Zani, Barbara
Zehntner, Rosemary
Zelick, Cheryl
Zelny, Sandra
Zidonik, Tara
Zimmermann, Mary B.
Zurka, Mary

PHOTO CREDITS

All photographs are from the WGAM Collection* with the exception of the following:

Front Cover: Mrs. Raymond July 1904, Copyright - Robert L. Stewart, Frame Central

<u>Introduction</u>: Jeanne-Marie Boylan, USGA

PART I – THE STORY
<u>The Beginning</u>.   14: Harriot Curtis, USGA; 15: Margaret Curtis, USGA

<u>The Early Years</u>. 21: Glenna Collett, USGA; 18: Fashion of the Day - Scituate Country Club, Moira McCarthy Collection

<u>World War II</u>. 27: Deborah Verry, WGAM from International News Photos <u>VICTOR AND RUNNER-UP IN PINEHURST TOURNEY</u>

<u>Mid-Century</u>. 34: Joanne Goodwin, USGA; 36: Joanne Goodwin and Barbara McIntyre, USGA

<u>Modern Times</u>. 50: Marion McInerney, USGA

<u>Champions, Legends, & Ambassadors</u>. 61: Glenna Collett Autograph, from WGAM copy of her book "Ladies in the Rough"; 62: Marion McInerney and Carol Semple Thompson, USGA; 63: Mildred Prunaret, USGA; 65: Mildred Prunaret, Boston Public Library Collection; 66: Frances Stebbins, USGA; 67: Florence McClusky, Boston Public Library Collection

PART TWO – THE CENTENNIAL CELEBRATION

104: The Country Club's 1951 W.G.A. First Cup Champions, Boston Public Library Collection; Spring Team Match 1st Cup Winners – Winchester Country Club, Russ Adam - *Boston Herald;* 125: Joanne Goodwin, USGA

ABOUT THE AUTHOR
158: Moira McCarthy, Anne D'Angelo

*The WGAM Collection includes several newspaper articles and clippings whose source is not known. In addition, many members (past and present) have donated photographs and clippings from their own personal collections which have become part of the WGAM Collection.

ABOUT THE AUTHOR
Part I - The Story

 Moira McCarthy is an internationally published magazine writer and author. A regular contributor to SKI, Tennis and FamilyLife Magazines, her work has also appeared in the New York Times, International Business Traveller and National Geographic, among others. A former nationally award winning investigative reporter and crime reporter, she lives in Plymouth, Massachusetts with her husband and two daughters. An avid skier and tennis player, she is currently working to improve her golf game at Waverly Oaks Golf Club in Plymouth. Mother of a child with Type 1 Diabetes, McCarthy is also a volunteer at the national level of the Juvenile Diabetes Research Foundation.